What to Do if You Were Left Behind After Rapture

By

Prophetess Mary J. Ogenaarekhua

Endorsement

"Millions are gone, vanished; family, friends, children and you heard about Rapture before it happened but it sounded too ridiculous to believe. Could it have really happened? What can you do, what must you do now?

If you are searching for the truth, you will discover it in the pages of, "*What to Do if You Were Left Behind After Rapture*" by Prophetess Mary O. **Widely accepted false beliefs are revealed and instructions are given that will place your destiny on the right path and keep it there.**

If you obtain a copy of this book before Rapture, it means you can read it to learn about the Lord's will for you and how to avoid the horror of being left behind. The most important choice you will ever make is now facing you.

> 'But I have prayed for thee, that thy faith fail not and when thou art converted, strengthen thy brethren' (Luke 22:32).'"

— Lynne Garbinsky

"Prophetess Mary's bold new book '*What to Do if You Were Left Behind After Rapture*' is an urgent and timely read for all Christians and especially those outside of the Christian faith. **The book gives a clear vision into the post Rapture world, exposes where many religions went wrong; even laying the groundwork and prayers to minister to those outside of the Christian Faith.**

Be prepared to be greatly blessed as you read and 'hear' the truths laid out in this book; they will provide you soul-saving direction as your faith is confronted in the days ahead. God Bless You."

— Teresa M, Atlanta, GA

Dedication

As with all my books, I dedicate this book to my heavenly Father, my Lord Jesus Christ and my Lord the Holy Spirit. LORD Jesus, You walked into my bedroom with a very delicate pen in your hand, sat by the head of my bed and gave me the words to write in this book. I thank You for it because without Your instructions, I will not have anything to write. I also thank You for telling me about the urgency of making this book available now and for giving me the grace to write what You taught me as it is written in **Psalm 68:11**:

> "**The Lord gave the word**: great was the company of those that published it."

LORD God, may this book bring You much glory and may You use it to bring Your children and those who desire to know You closer to You. I ask for your forgiveness if any words that I used in this book come across to anyone as harsh. I am sorry for it because you commanded me to be very delicate in the words that I used in this book.

I also dedicate this book to faithful believers who have been trying to tell their loved ones and others about the need to accept the Lord Jesus to no avail. Now, you can leave a copy of this book behind for them to read. I pray they take heed to what is written in it.

Finally, I dedicate this book to all the Great Tribulation Saints. Know that the Lord wants you to be with Him in heaven and you will learn how to get to Him in the pages of this book.

What to Do if You Were Left Behind After Rapture

Unless otherwise indicated, all scriptures are quoted
from the <u>King James Version</u> of the Bible.

Published by: To His Glory Publishing Company, Inc.
(770) 458-7947
www.tohisglorypublishing.com

This Book is available at:
Amazon.com, BarnesandNoble.com, Booksamillion.com,
and in the UK, EU, Canada, Australia, etc.
See Prophetess Mary's teachings at youtube.com/c/maryjministries

Also call or email below to order this book.
(770) 458-7947
www.tohisglorypublishing.com
Email: tohisglorypublishing@yahoo.com
Published May 2023

ISBN: 978-1-942724-09-4

Table of Contents

Preface

"This book is meant for **all Christians to leave <u>behind before Rapture</u>** for their **loved ones who are not currently living for Christ**. It is mainly for **'Christians' who have missed Rapture** *(left behind)* and are now **faced** with a **'New World Order' under the reign of the antichrist** and the **false prophet**.

It is also for **people who were practicing different religions before Rapture occurred, who want to know what happened and what else will happen on earth.** It will be an **eye-opener** for anyone who reads it and now wants to commit his or her life to the Lord Jesus Christ. **<u>It contains guidelines for making Jesus your Lord</u>.**"

—**Prophetess Mary J. Ogenaarekhua**

Acknowledgements

Heavenly Father, I acknowledge the gift of a Scribe that you have given me and I thank You for fulfilling Your Word to me through Your Son, my Lord Jesus Christ that:

> **"Every scribe which is instructed unto the kingdom of heaven** is like unto a man that is an <u>householder</u>, **which bringeth forth out of his <u>treasure</u> things new and old"** (Matthew 13:52).

I thank my mother, **Dr. Patricia Gbadamosi** who stressed to me the importance of leading people in the 'Prayer of Salvation.'

Thank you **Lynne Garbinsky** for helping me proofread, edit and layout this book. You are a steadfast soldier and may the Lord bless you beyond your imagination.

I also thank **Teresa M.** who put hours and days into helping me to edit this book. May the Lord greatly reward you. You are a blessing.

Introduction

The Lord Jesus instructed me to write this book for those who were <u>Left Behind after Rapture</u>. Therefore, if you are <u>blessed to come across a copy of this book</u> before **Rapture** occurred, I hope that you take heed to what is written in it and as such are <u>not left behind</u>.

On the other hand, if you are reading it <u>after Rapture</u>, it means that you have been left behind so <u>please</u>, pay attention to the topics addressed in it. They will encourage and **<u>help you find your way to the Lord Jesus</u>** as well as tell you what to do in the '**new world**' that you now find yourself.

To begin with, **I do not have to <u>convince you that God's Word in the Bible is the only truth there is</u>** because you are **seeing the after effects of what the Word of God said will happen after the Lord comes and removes all the faithful Christians at Rapture.** As the **Bible** said, you are now living in a chaotic world full of wicked men and women who only care about themselves.

Also, know that <u>God's Word supersedes</u> everything that you will read or hear from the leaders of your 'New World.' Be assured that **<u>it is not too late for you if your faith is now steadfast in Christ being your Lord</u>**.

I say to you upfront that, as a **Christian** in your '**New World**,' you might **<u>get persecuted</u>** by the forces of the antichrist *(the world leader that will arise)*, but **do not despair**. As a matter of fact, the **Bible** tells us that, **<u>many Christians will be targeted when they refuse to renounce their faith in Christ</u>**. Be determined to **hold on to the Word of God and <u>do not compromise your faith</u>** no matter what. Your **<u>guiding spiritual principle</u>** should now be the Lord's Word in **Luke 12:4-5:**

> "And I say unto you <u>my friends</u>, **Be not <u>afraid</u> of them that <u>kill the body, and after that have no</u>**

> <u>**more that they can do.**</u> 5 But **I will <u>forewarn</u> you whom ye shall fear**: <u>Fear him</u> *(God)*, <u>**which after he hath killed hath power to cast into hell**</u>**; yea, I say unto you, <u>Fear him</u>**."

Regardless of what is going on in your world, do not fear what a man can do to you because **as the Lord Jesus** said in the scripture above, **they cannot kill your Soul which is <u>what really matters.</u>** God will give you a new body in Christ when the one you are now in is destroyed by the wicked men in your new world. **It is <u>where your soul will spend eternity</u> that you should now be concerned about. <u>Settle it in your heart that you might lose your life</u>** in the times you are living. Therefore, walk as such but not **foolishly** or **presumptuously**.

If you have not been calling on the name of the Lord, now is the time to call on the Lord Jesus. Again, do not despair but be sober and be vigilant as you trust the Lord daily. **Get a copy of the New King James Bible. I quoted a lot of scriptural references from the King James Bible (KJV) for you in this book just in case the Bible is now hard to come by.**

WARNING:
Do not renounce Christ no matter what
Do not kill yourself: See page 131 for detailed discussion

Chapter 1
Were You Left Behind after Rapture?

Definition of Rapture

Rapture is the instance of someone or something **ceasing to be visible**; vanished to the naked eye. In Christianity, **Rapture** is called, **"being caught-up"** to **meet the Lord in the sky**; the sudden **disappearance of faithful Christians and children** from all over the world. It means the Lord Jesus' **'Taking Away His Church'** *(those who believed in Him)*. In a nutshell, Rapture is the fulfillment of the Lord's promise to the believers in **John 14:1-3:**

> "Let not your heart be troubled: ye believe in God, believe also in me. 2 **In my Father's house are many mansions: if it were not so, I would have told you. I go to prepare a place for you. 3 And if I go and prepare a place for you, <u>I will come again, and receive you unto myself</u>; that where I am, there ye may be also."**

It means that those who **believed and walked faithfully** with the Lord Jesus Christ were **taken away from the earth to be with Him in Heaven.** The Apostle Paul wrote about "**being caught up**" *(Rapture)* in **1 Thessalonians 4:13-18:**

> "But I would not have you to be ignorant, brethren, concerning them which are asleep, that ye sorrow not, even as others which have no hope. 14 **For if we believe that Jesus died and rose again, even so them also which sleep in Jesus will God bring with him.**
>
> 15 For this we say unto you by the word of the Lord, that we which are alive and remain unto the coming of the Lord shall not prevent them which are asleep. 16 **For the Lord himself shall descend from heaven with a shout, with the voice of the**

archangel, and with the trump of God: and the dead in Christ shall rise first:

17 Then we which are alive and remain shall be caught up together with them in the clouds, to meet the Lord in the air: and so shall we ever be with the Lord. 18 Wherefore comfort one another with these words."

He repeated it in **1 Corinthians 15:50-55:**

"Now this I say, brethren, that **flesh and blood cannot inherit the kingdom of God; neither doth corruption inherit incorruption.** 51 Behold, I shew you a mystery; **We shall not all sleep, but we shall all be changed,**

52 **In a moment, in the twinkling of an eye, at the last trump: for the trumpet shall sound, and the dead shall be raised incorruptible, and we shall be changed.** 53 For this corruptible must put on incorruption, and this mortal must put on immortality.

54 So when this corruptible shall have put on incorruption, and this mortal shall have put on immortality, then shall be brought to pass the saying that is written, Death is swallowed up in victory. 55 O death, where is thy sting? O grave, where is thy victory?"

The Occurrence of Rapture

Regardless of your religion, if you were **left behind**, you know by now that faithful **Christians** and **children** have **suddenly disappeared all over the world.** The 'Christians' who were left behind understand what happened while non-Christians are wondering what happened; crying for their babies and loved ones that suddenly disappeared. Many **who rejected Christian evangelists** that tried to tell them that **Jesus is the only person that can save them** are now either blaming themselves or are seeking answers to what happened. As a result, many of them **will come to question their non-Christian religions and beliefs**.

What the Sudden Disappearance of Millions Proved to the World

The sudden disappearance or Rapture proved to the world that **Jesus Christ is who He said He is—the Son of God!** Again, it proved that **the Lord Jesus has kept His promise to come back and take His Church out of this world** *(those who were faithful to Him)* as He promised.

It also proved that as the Lord said in **John 14:6, He is the only way that anyone can get to God:**

> "Jesus saith unto him, I am the **way**, the **truth**, and the **life**: **no man cometh unto the Father, but by Me.**"

Rapture is an **attestation** of God's Word in **John 3:16-19** which says that **whoever believes in God's Son; Jesus Christ, shall be saved** and **whoever does not believe** shall be **condemned**:

> **"For God so loved the world that he gave his only begotten Son, that whosoever believeth in him should not perish, but have everlasting life.** *17* For God sent not his Son into the world **to condemn** the world; but that **the world through him might be saved.**
>
> *18* **He that believeth on him is not condemned**: but **he that believeth not is condemned already, because he hath not believed in the name of the only begotten Son of God.** *19* And **this is the condemnation, that light is come into the world,** and **men loved darkness** rather **than light,** because **their deeds were evil.**"

Why Did God Take the Children?

Remember that when Jesus Christ was physically here on earth, **He preached to parents with little children. Children**

are born innocent just as Adam and Eve were, **until they get corrupted by sin.** While children are **still innocent, God protects and keeps** them but when they <u>start</u> **to lie and to hide their wrong doings, they lose their innocence.**

Every **child reaches this stage of covering up wrong doing at a different age.** A good example is the cookie jar. When a child is **young and innocent** and the mother tells the child to stay away from the cookie jar, the child might go and take a cookie and eat it. When the mother comes and sees cookie crumbs on the face of the child and she asks the child if he took a cookie from the jar, **the child smiles and says no without realizing that the evidence of his actions are all over his face.**

As this same child gets older and learns that disobedience has consequences, when the mother tells the child to stay out of the **cookie jar** and he disobeys, **takes a cookie but carefully rearranges the cookies in the jar so that the mother will not know that a cookie is missing. Also, the child carefully wipes his face so that there is no evidence of what he did. This age that the** <u>child knows to cover up his actions and lie about it is</u> called the '<u>Age of Accountability</u>.' The action of the child proves that the child does not want to be held accountable for his disobedience by covering up the evidence. This action (sin), means that **the child now knows the difference between right and wrong.** People get to this stage of lying at different ages and God sees it all from Heaven; He knows when the child stops being innocent.

Unfortunately, when this happens, **sin** (*wrong doing*) **separates them from God's Presence. Therefore, at Rapture, the Lord only took the children that have not yet learned how to cover up their wrong doing;** they do not know sin.

What the Lord Jesus Said About the Little Children

The Lord Jesus cares about the little children because they are all innocent and they have a relationship with God the Father. This is what He said concerning them in **Matthew 18:10**:

"Take heed that ye despise not one of these little ones; for I say unto you, **That in heaven their angels** *(spirits)* <u>do always behold the face of my Father</u> which is in heaven."

Also, in **Mark 10:15**, He said:

"Verily I say unto you, **Whosoever shall not receive the kingdom of God** <u>as a little child</u>, he shall not enter therein."

This is revealed again in **Matthew 19:13-14:**

"Then were there brought unto him little children, that he should put his hands on them, and pray: and the disciples rebuked them. *14* But Jesus said, **Suffer** <u>little children, and forbid them not, to come unto me:</u> for of such is the kingdom of heaven. *15* And **he laid his hands on them,** and departed thence."

He also said in **Matthew 18:14:**

"Even so <u>it is not the will of your Father which is in heaven,</u> that <u>one of these little ones should perish.</u>"

You see, God did not want the little children to perish. **He took them and did not leave them behind to suffer His wrath that will come upon the earth**.

Do Not Believe the Lies of World Leaders about Rapture

Governments of different nations are right now **lying to their citizens by giving them false narratives about the Rapture**. Some are contending that:

1. It **never really happened**; it is not a Christian event
2. That **aliens came and took away** the 'undesirables'
3. Others are saying that **some natural phenomenon happened that resulted in disappearance of millions of people**

You are right now having a front row seat to all these. **Do not buy into their lies but be fully persuaded that it was a work of God.**

Rapture is not the Work of UFOs

World leaders and many people will **try to explain away Rapture as the work of Extraterrestrial beings;** do not believe them. Even some **'apostate left behind church leaders,' those who were not faithful in their Christian walk, scientists, so-called UFO trackers,** etc., **will offer you man-made 'proofs'** of what they **claim happened** but know that **they will all be lies to pacify you.** The **spirit of deception and delusion will come upon these people** to make them believe in their own lies — **2 Thessalonians 2:9-11:**

> "Even him *(antichrist)*, whose coming is after the working of Satan with all power and signs and lying wonders, *10* And with all deceivableness of unrighteousness **in them that perish;** because they received not the love of the truth, that they might be saved. *11* And **for this cause God shall send them strong delusion, that they should believe a lie.**"

Be assured that **the occurrence of Rapture is the work of God** as foretold in the Bible. I also want you to know that according to the Bible, 7 years after Rapture, **the Lord Jesus will come back** with **all the Christians who had died before Rapture occurred** and **all those who were 'caught up' at Rapture.** Everyone on earth will see them when they descend from Heaven to earth! He will come to execute His judgment on all those who rejected Him. We first read this in **Jude 1:14-15:**

> "And Enoch also, the seventh from Adam, prophesied of these, saying, **Behold, the Lord cometh with ten thousands of his saints,** *15* To execute judgment upon all, and to convince all that are ungodly among them of all their ungodly

deeds which they have ungodly committed, and of all their hard speeches which ungodly sinners have spoken against him."

And also in **Revelation 1:7:**

"Behold, he cometh with clouds; and every eye shall see him, and they also which pierced him *(crucified Him; Israel):* and **all kindreds of the earth shall wail because of him**. Even so, Amen."

Every person on earth will **cry out and wail because they did not place their trust in Christ;** they will **greatly regret their actions** but it will be too late for them. The **Millennial Reign of Christ on earth** is recorded in **Revelations 20:6:**

"**Blessed and holy is he that hath part in the first resurrection** *(all the Christians who died or were raptured):* **on such the second death hath no power** *(a life in hell),* but **they shall be priests of God and of Christ,** and **shall reign with him a thousand years.**"

Again, know that **world leaders and their governments will try to blame Rapture on aliens or come up with some ungodly explanations but do not believe them.** Get a copy of the **Bible** and read about **Rapture** for yourself.

Chapter 2
Some of the Reasons Why You Were Left Behind

Definition of Left Behind

Being **left behind means to miss Rapture and you were not taken** when the Lord Jesus Christ came and took away His Church from the earth. Since you were left behind after the Rapture, it means that **you need God and the salvation that is in His Son; the Lord Jesus Christ now more than ever**.

The reason for **your critical need for Christ now** is because major calamities will come upon the earth along with all those in it and only God can help those who believe and trust in Him. Unfortunately, you will go through some of these **calamities that will befall the people on earth but the Lord can help you when you call upon Him.**

The subtitles in this chapter address what those who were left behind **failed to understand** as being very important to their souls. Hopefully as you read them, you will change your attitude, beliefs and trust the Lord with your soul. This means that you need to review your life and see where you went wrong.

The Importance of the Cross

The people that the Lord took away to Heaven in **Rapture were all those who believed in Him, trusted in Him and lived their lives according to His will and not their own.** Therefore, if you were left behind, do not get angry at God because it is not His fault that you were not taken. **He gave you years and countless opportunities to come to Him through Jesus Christ, His Son but you did not heed His call or know the importance of the Cross to your soul due to some of the reasons listed below.**

1. Your **unbelief**; you did not believe or receive the Gospel about Christ

2. You **professed to believe** but did not really commit yourself to Him
3. You **compromised your Christian walk**; lived like the world
4. You **were** *(no offense)*, **a hypocrite** *(meaning, you say but do not do)*
5. You **followed your pastor** instead of Christ
6. You **were too busy for God**
7. You **thought you had more time** before accepting Christ or changing your lifestyle
8. You **thought you knew better than God**
9. You **thought you were wiser than God** because of your PhDs
10. You **insisted on living your life according to your own will**; God calls this iniquity
11. You **chose to live a lifestyle that God calls <u>abominable</u>** *(homosexual, deviant and oral sex)*
12. You **chose to <u>remake yourself in your own image</u>**; sex or gender change, plastic surgery, changed your skin color, etc.
13. You **were a satanist**; openly worshipped satan, belonged to a cult, practiced witchcraft
14. You **worshipped satan** through idolatry and false doctrines
15. You **practiced a pagan religion**
16. You **refused to convert** to Christianity from your false religion

There are many more reasons but **only you know your personal reason which the Bible calls <u>the sin that easily besets you</u> in Hebrews 12:1:**

> "Wherefore seeing we also are compassed about with so great a cloud of witnesses, let us lay aside every weight, and **the sin which doth so easily beset us**, and let us run with patience the race that is set before us…"

I have tried to outline below from God's perspective, some of the **major life changing knowledge and decisions that most of the people left behind failed to pay attention to throughout their lives.** Now is the time to rethink your decisions and make a change.

Christ is All You Need for Righteousness

In Christendom, **righteousness** is defined as **having our sins forgiven by God so that we are in right standing with Him**; meaning we stand before Him having our sins washed by the Blood of Jesus Christ, His Son. It means that God declared us 'not guilty' of our sins because Christ paid for them with His life and we received it; not because of our good works. God does not want anyone to rely on his or her own righteousness but to know that **Christ is ALL that we require to be righteous before God** if we obey His Word. **Our Salvation is not based on our good works but on our faith in Christ**. Although God expects us to **do good works** after our salvation *(being Born Again)*, but **good works are not what makes us righteous — Romans 10:3-4:**

> "For they *(Israel and all unbelievers)* **being ignorant of God's righteousness**, and going about to establish their own righteousness, have not submitted themselves unto the righteousness of God. 4 **For Christ is the end of the law for righteousness** to everyone that believeth.**"

We are again told in **Galatians 2:16** that we cannot achieve righteousness with our good works. God will never regard anyone as righteous based on what the person did but by faith in His Son Jesus Christ:

> "Knowing that **a man is not justified by the works of the law, but <u>by the faith of Jesus Christ</u>**, even we have believed in Jesus Christ, that **we might be justified by the faith of Christ**, and not by the works of the law: **for by the works of the law shall no flesh be justified.**"

Righteousness is a gift from God that we cannot buy or earn because of our good behavior. We cannot achieve righteousness by ourselves. God regards our individual righteousness as "**filthy rags**" in **Isaiah 64:6:**

> "But **we are all as an unclean thing**, and **<u>all our righteousnesses are as filthy rags</u>**; and we all do

fade as a leaf; and **our iniquities, like the wind,** have taken us away."

You must place your trust in Christ even after Rapture because **He can still save those left behind that place their trust in Him.** He is that much of a God and a Savior that receives all who trust Him with their lives. This is why **the hope of those who trust in the Lord during the Great Tribulation is revealed in Revelation 15:2-4:**

> "And I saw as it were a sea of glass mingled with fire: and them *(Christians after Rapture)* that **had gotten the victory over the beast, and over his image, and over his mark, and over the number of his name**, stand on the sea of glass, having the harps of God.
>
> 3 And **they sing the song of Moses the servant of God, and the song of the Lamb**, saying, Great and marvellous are thy works, Lord God Almighty; just and true are thy ways, thou King of saints. 4 Who shall not fear thee, O Lord, and glorify thy name? for thou only art holy: **for all nations shall come and worship before thee; for thy judgments are made manifest.**"

Man's History with God Concerning Sin

The truth is that God created **Man** *(Adam and Eve)* **as innocent beings** before placing man in **the Garden of Eden** but, the devil in the form of a serpent **deceived man to rebel against God.** Both **Adam and Eve along with all their descendants** *(all humanity)*, were **separated from God** due to this sin which we call the '**original sin**' as we see in **Genesis 3:22-24** below. I will discuss this in detail in *Chapter 4* titled, *'The Beginning of God's Problem with Sin and Man.'*

> "And the LORD God said, **Behold, the man is become as one of us, to know good and evil:** and now, lest he put forth his hand, and take also of the tree of life, and eat, and live forever:

23 **Therefore the LORD God sent him forth from the Garden of Eden,** to till the ground from whence he was taken. 24 **So he drove out the man; and he placed at the east of the garden of Eden Cherubims,** and a flaming sword which turned every way, to keep the way of the tree of life."

As I stated above, **Adam and Eve passed this <u>sin and its nature</u> to every human being** (*their descendants*)**.** Adam and Eve willfully chose the devil's lying and sinful nature by obeying him instead of God. This is why **you do not have to teach a child how to lie;** the devil makes sure that it **comes naturally to him or her because lying** (*sin*) is the nature of the devil. Therefore, God **concluded all humanity to be guilty of this 'Sin of Rebellion'** against Him — **Romans 3:23:**

"For **all have sinned,** and **come short of the glory of God**..."

It is repeated in **Romans 3:10-12:**

"...**There is none righteous, no, not one:** 11 There is none that understandeth, **there is none that seeketh after God.** 12 They are all gone out of the way, they are together become unprofitable; **there is none that doeth good, no, not one.**"

Sinful man has been looking for ways to get back to God by <u>inventing pagan religions</u> and trying to appease God to no avail. Because the devil knows that God hates idolatry, he made sure that all of man's religious efforts all over the world to reach God were idolatry that he inspired so that he can receive '**proxy worship'** from man.

God's Mercy towards Man (*You*) in Christ

Since there was **no way for sinful man to get back to the Most Holy and Righteous God, God Himself came down to earth in His Word** (*Jesus*) **to save us.** In other words, God in His Mercy sent His Son our **Lord Jesus Christ to become Man and pay for our sin on the Cross** as it is written in **John 3:16-18:**

"For God so loved the world, that he gave his only begotten Son, that whosoever believeth in him should not perish, but have everlasting life. 17 For God sent not his Son into the world to condemn the world; but that the world through him might be saved.

18 He that believeth on him is not condemned: but he that believeth not is condemned already, because he hath not believed in the name of the only begotten Son of God."

This is why the Lord Jesus wants you to know that **He is the only way** to God when He said in **John 14:6:**

"…I am the Way, the Truth, and the Life: no man cometh unto the Father, but by Me."

There is no way to be free from sin outside of the Lord Jesus Christ.

Faith and Repentance are Required to Receive Christ's Finished Works

The **finished Works of Christ** *(the Cross)*, **God's free gift of salvation** is still available to both the **Jews** and the **Gentiles** even after Rapture! We are **not required to bring God anything but faith to receive the free gift of His Son** as we see in **Romans 10:8-9:**

"But what saith it? The word is nigh thee, even in thy mouth, and in thy heart: that is, the word of faith, which we preach; 9 **That if thou shalt confess with thy mouth the Lord Jesus, and shalt believe in thine heart that God hath raised him from the dead, thou shalt be saved.**"

The reason **God only requires faith** is because **He has done for you in His Son, all that He needs for you to be saved from sin.** Before the Lord Jesus went to the Cross to die for our sins, **there was no way for any man to approach or stand before God without sin.** It was the reason why the Apostle

John '**wept much**' as recorded in **Revelation 5:1-6** when he saw that **there was no one worthy to stand before God to pronounce God's judgment on sin and the devil in order to free humanity from the devil's bondage or grip on mankind through sin:**

> "And I saw in the right hand of him that sat on the throne a book written within and on the backside, sealed with seven seals. 2 And I saw a strong angel proclaiming with a loud voice, Who is worthy to open the book, and to loose the seals thereof? 3 And no man in heaven, nor in earth, neither under the earth, was able to open the book, neither to look thereon.
>
> 4 And I **wept much, because no man was found worthy to open and to read the book, neither to look thereon.** 5 And one of the elders saith unto me, **Weep not**: behold, **the Lion of the tribe of Juda, the Root of David, hath prevailed to open the book, and to loose the seven seals thereof.**
>
> 6 And I beheld, and, lo, in the midst of the throne and of the four beasts, and in the midst of the elders, **stood a Lamb as it had been slain,** having seven horns and seven eyes, which are the seven Spirits of God sent forth into all the earth."

Again, **to receive God's free gift of salvation,** you must **believe His Gospel** or **Good News** preached to you as written in **1 Corinthians 1:18-24.** Some people regard **the preaching of the Gospel as foolish** but to those who believe in Christ, **it is the power of God:**

> "For the preaching of the cross is to **them that perish foolishness; but unto us which are saved it is the power of God.** 19 For it is written, **I will destroy the wisdom of the wise, and will bring to nothing the understanding of the prudent.** 20 Where is the wise? where is the scribe? where is the disputer of this world? hath not God made foolish the wisdom of this world?

31

21 **For after that in the wisdom of God the world by wisdom knew not God, it pleased God by the foolishness of preaching to save them that believe.** 22 **For the Jews require a sign,** and the **Greeks seek after wisdom:** 23 **But we preach Christ crucified,** unto the **Jews a stumblingblock,** and unto the **Greeks foolishness;** 24 **But unto them which are called, both Jews and Greeks, Christ the power of God, and the wisdom of God."**

He expects you to believe that Jesus is His Son and that He died for your sin. It does not matter what religion you were raised in because **God expects you to believe the Good News that His Son died for your sin and to shift your belief to His Son.** You must receive His Son and then live by His Word to be saved so that God does not have to condemn you to hell.

About Your World Right Now

You have now awakened into a new world and a 'New World Order.' Therefore, you **must make a decision about your life, religious beliefs,** allegiance to your government, world leaders and their new behaviors. Above all, you must hold onto your faith in Christ even if it costs you your earthly life. If you do, you will spend eternity with God the Father, the Lord Jesus Christ, the Lord Holy Spirit and all the Saints in Heaven.

Now is the time to <u>focus on the things that have eternal value;</u> where your Soul will dwell for all of eternity. You were left behind the first time so do not miss this last chance of being rescued from hell by Christ because all who do will be condemned forever.

Occurrence of Rapture is Your Great Evangelism Tool

At this point, **you need to change your attitude about having been <u>left behind</u> because, there is so much you can do for God right now.** Many people like you missed Him and were also left behind at Rapture. It is now your job to witness to them if you choose to accept it; live your life for Christ. You can help many to not miss Him forever. Your message is to let them know that all those left behind who put their trust in Christ can still be saved by Him even if they are killed physically.

You are to help them to know the danger of the second death; eternal separation from God in hell. They need to know that they still have so much to gain by believing in Christ right now and His Words in **Matthew 10:24-28** should now resonate in their minds everyday:

> **"The disciple is not above his master, nor the servant above his lord.** 25 **It is enough for the disciple that he be as his master, and the servant as his lord** *(He was killed)*. If they have called the master of the house Beelzebub, how much more shall they call them of his household?
>
> 26 **Fear them not therefore**: for there is nothing covered, that shall not be revealed; and hid, that shall not be known... 28 **And fear not them which kill the body, but are not able to kill the soul: but rather fear him which is able to destroy both soul and body in hell."**

And in **Luke 9:25**, He asked:

> **"For what is a man advantaged, if he gain the whole world, and lose himself, or be cast away?"**

Some Biblical Scriptures that Explain the Disappearance of Many

John 14:1-3:

> "Let not your heart be troubled: ye believe in God, believe also in me. 2 In my Father's house are many mansions: if it were not so, I would have told you. **I go to prepare a place for you.** 3 And if I go and prepare a place for you, **I will come again, and receive you unto myself; that where I am, there ye may be also."**

I Thessalonians 4:14-18:

"For if we believe that Jesus died and rose again, even so them also which sleep in Jesus will God bring with him. 15 For this we say unto you by the word of the Lord, that we which are alive and remain unto the coming of the Lord shall not prevent them which are asleep. **16 For the Lord himself shall descend from heaven with a shout, with the voice of the archangel, and with the trump of God: and the dead in Christ shall rise first: 17 Then we which are alive and remain shall be caught up together with them in the clouds, to meet the Lord in the air**: and so shall we ever be with the Lord. 18 Wherefore comfort one another with these words."

1 Corinthians 15:51-53:

"Behold, I shew you a mystery; We shall not all sleep *(die)*, but we shall all be changed, **52 In a moment, in the twinkling of an eye, at the last trump**: for the trumpet shall sound, and **the dead shall be** raised **incorruptible, and we shall be changed. 53 For this corruptible must put on incorruption, and this mortal must put on immortality.**"

Biblical Definitions of Terms Used in the Book

Repent – willingness to forsake sin and ask God for forgiveness

Antichrist or Beast – the coming new world leader

False Prophet – spokesperson for the Beast

Tribulation – time after Rapture filled with trials ending with the Lord's Second Coming

Note: Make sure you read this book in its entirety to learn what to do and how to apply God's principles to your life.

Chapter 3
State of the World Before Rapture Occurred

The World was Only Concerned with Secular Knowledge

Scriptures tell us that **before the Lord comes back to take His Church away** *(those who believed and lived according to His Word)*, **the <u>world will become a wicked and immoral place</u>**. Truly, the world became concerned with secular knowledge (worldly knowledge) at the expense of Godly Knowledge.

Many people **discarded** or **turned their backs** on God's instructions as they chose to follow what they called, 'the Science.' They also had a great **intolerance of God, His Word, His children and they <u>despised and mocked the Wisdom</u> that comes from God and His Word**. They called Christian Evangelists undesirables and parts of the Bible obscured and archaic.

The Working of a Reprobate Mind

As a result of people turning their backs on God and pursuing only wickedness, they became **spiritually blind to <u>anything good and of eternal value</u>. Therefore, God in turn gave them over** to what is called a **'Reprobate Mind.' A reprobate mind is a <u>depraved mind</u>; a morally corrupt or wicked mind. Secular knowledge does not produce godly wisdom but leads to a 'Reprobate Mind.'** We see this outlined in **Romans 1:18-32**:

> "For **the <u>wrath of God</u> is revealed from heaven against all ungodliness and unrighteousness of men, who hold the truth in unrighteousness**; *19* **Because that which may be known of God is manifest in them; for God hath shewed it unto them**. *20* <u>For the invisible things of him from the creation of the world are clearly seen</u>, **being understood by the things that are made** *(a look at creation will tell you that someone designed it; it does not take a genius to know)*, **even his <u>eternal power and Godhead</u>; so that they are without excuse:**

21 Because that, **when they knew God, they glorified him not as God, neither were thankful;** but **became vain in their imaginations,** and **their foolish heart was darkened**. 22 **Professing themselves to be wise, they became fools,** 23 And changed the glory of the uncorruptible God into an image made like to corruptible man, and to birds, and fourfooted beasts, and creeping things *(idol worshippers)*.

24 Wherefore **God also gave them up to uncleanness through the lusts of their own hearts,** to **dishonour their own bodies between themselves** *(homosexuals):* 25 Who changed the truth of God into a lie, and worshipped and served the creature *(earth worshipers)* more than the Creator, who is blessed forever. Amen. 26 **For this cause God gave them up unto vile affections**: for **even their women did change the natural use into that which is against nature** *(lesbians):*

27 And **likewise also the men, leaving the natural use of the woman, burned in their lust one toward another; men with men working that which is unseemly,** and **receiving in themselves that recompence of their error which was meet** *(deserved).* 28 And even as they did not like to retain God in their knowledge, **God gave them over to a Reprobate Mind,** to do those things which are not convenient;

29 **Being filled with** all **unrighteousness, fornication, wickedness, covetousness, maliciousness;** full of **envy, murder,** debate *(instead of having faith),* **deceit, malignity; whisperers** *(gossipers),* 30 **Backbiters, haters of God, despiteful, proud, boasters, inventors of evil things, disobedient to parents,** 31 **Without understanding, covenantbreakers** *(do not keep their word),* **without natural affection, implacable, unmerciful**:

32 Who knowing the judgment of God, that **they which commit such things are worthy of death**, not only do the same, **but have pleasure in them that do them** *(those who support them)."*

Also, concerning **the workings of the Reprobate Mind**, the Word of God says this in **2 Timothy 3:1-8:**

"This know also, that **in the last days perilous times shall come**. 2 For men shall be **lovers of their own selves, covetous, boasters, proud, blasphemers, disobedient to parents, unthank-ful, unholy**, 3 **Without natural affection, truce-breakers, false accusers, incontinent** *(never satisfied),* **fierce, despisers of those that are good,**

4 **Traitors, heady, highminded, lovers of pleasures more than lovers of God;** 5 **Having a form of godliness, but denying the power thereof** *(the apostate church)*: from such turn away... **Ever learning, and never able to come to the knowledge of the truth.** 8 Now as Jannes and Jambres withstood Moses, **so do these also resist the truth**: **men of corrupt minds, Reprobate concerning the faith**."

What was Important to World Leaders

If world leaders, financial movers and shakers were as **concerned about God and His Ways** as they were about 'Climate Change,' 'Saving the earth' and population control *(their 'New Gospel')*, the world you now find yourself living in would have been a **much better place**. Instead, **all on earth are facing God's wrath** and you are living in a world where the **minds of the ungodly** became **reprobate** when:

1. **They fought** and **openly opposed God** and His ways
2. **They overthrew all of God's standards** in the family, gender and society
3. **They claimed men can have babies**
4. **They fought for the right to be openly perverted** and then

they legislated it

5. **They went insane over the right to kill innocent babies** in the womb
6. **They were hell bent on** <u>remaking themselves</u> **in their own image** while rejecting their God-assigned genders
7. **They hated what is good and godly** but delighted themselves in evil
8. **They called evil good and good evil**
9. **They persecuted** those who do not buy into their insanity

This is why **God gave them over** to a **Reprobate Mind** since they **did not like to retain God in their knowledge**. In the new world that you now found yourself, be careful of <u>who and what you support;</u> **you do not want to be condemned with the ones that still reject God and pledge their allegiance to the antichrist.**

News Headlines before Rapture Occurred

You can now remember what the news headlines were before Rapture occurred but for those who were looking forward to the Rapture, they saw what the **scriptures told us will happen being announced daily as headline news**. Faithful Christians saw the daily news report that the <u>reprobates have totally sold themselves to evil</u> as they:

1. **Threw out all moral values**
2. **Cast God's Word** and **standards** behind them
3. **Only cared for the life they were living** and not believing in eternal consequences
4. **Kicked against God's definition of the family**
5. **Kicked against His definition of gender** and came up with their own gender identities and pronouns
6. **Had no love for anyone else** except themselves
7. **Did not know what it means to forgive**
8. **Sought to rewrite history and the Bible**

The Results of a Society Full of Reprobates:

You are now living in a **society full of leaders and people who are proud, selfish, money lovers** and are **indulging in all form of wickedness and perversions. A society that** still:

- **Despises the truth** and **promotes lies** and **evil**
- Supports **heartless killers, rapists** and **looters**
- Supports **baby killers**
- Supports **parent killers**
- Supports **spouse** and **children killers**
- **Persecutes Christians** and **anything moral**
- Boldly **worships satan**

The Answer to a Reprobate Mind is Christ

Now, it is your job to tell those who are like minded as you that the **answer** to a **reprobate mind is Jesus Christ**. Tell them that only a **belief in Christ and His Word can produce the 'Mind of Christ'** which **pleases God** and that can **obey God**. All who reject Christ will become delusional and walk with a reprobate mind. This means a carnal mind that cannot please God as we see in **1 Corinthians 2:12-14**:

> "**Now we have received, not the spirit of the world, but the spirit which is of God**; that we might know the things that are freely given to us of God. 13 Which things also we speak, not in the words which man's wisdom teacheth, but which the Holy Ghost teacheth; comparing spiritual things with spiritual. 14 **But the natural man receiveth not the things of the Spirit of God: for they are foolishness unto him: neither can he know them**, because they are spiritually discerned."

The World Became as the Days of Noah

The **Lord Jesus said** that the **last days** (*days before His return*) would be like the **days of Noah** and the **days of Lot** in **Luke 17:26-30:**

> "And **as it was in the days of Noe** *(Noah),* **so shall it be also in the days of the Son of man. 27 They did eat, they drank**, they **married wives,** they **were given in marriage, until the day that Noe entered into the ark, and the flood came, and destroyed them all.**

28 Likewise also as it was in the days of Lot; they **did eat**, they **drank**, they **bought**, they **sold**, they **planted**, they **builded**; 29 But **the same day that Lot went out of Sodom** it **rained fire and brimstone from heaven, and destroyed them all.** 30 **Even thus shall it be in the day when the Son of man is revealed.**"

How Were the Days of Noah?

To know what was happening in the days of Noah, we have to look at **Genesis 6:5-7** because it tells us **about the behaviors of the men and women at that time. God had to bring His Judgment against them because** they only loved to do evil. Their wickedness was great upon the earth:

"And **GOD saw that the wickedness of man was great in the earth,** and that every imagination of the thoughts of his heart was only evil continually. 6 And it repented the LORD that he had made man on the earth, and it grieved him at his heart.

7 And the LORD said, **I will destroy man whom I have created from the face of the earth;** both **man,** and **beast,** and the **creeping thing,** and the **fowls of the air;** for **it repenteth me that I have made them.**"

Do you see why God brought a flood to kill all that dwelt on earth in the days of Noah? He did not hold back His Judgment as **He only saved Noah and his family** *(8 people)* out of the entire world population!

How Were the Days of Lot?

The men and women living in the days of Lot did not learn from God's Judgment upon those who lived in the days of Noah. **Their abominable lifestyle was an offense to God.** They not only debased their bodies but were vile in their ways to the point that they demanded that Lot bring out the two angels that were lodging in his house for them to sodomize! We are **told the following about the men of Sodom in Genesis 13:13:**

"But the men of Sodom were wicked and sinners before the LORD exceedingly."

And in **Genesis 19:3-5:**

"And he *(Lot)* pressed upon them *(angels)* greatly; and they turned in unto him, and entered into his house *(the angels became his guests for the night);* and he made them a feast, and did bake unleavened bread, and they did eat. 4 **But before they lay down, the men of the city, even the men of Sodom, compassed the house round, both old and young, all the people from every quarter:** 5 And they called unto Lot, and said unto him, **Where are the men which came in to thee this night? bring them out unto us, that we may know them** *(have homosexual acts with them)."*

We also learned the following about the **men of Sodom** in **2 Peter 2:6-8:**

"And **turning the cities** of **Sodom** and **Gomorrha** into ashes **condemned them with an overthrow,** making them an **ensample** unto those that **After should live ungodly;** 7 And **delivered just Lot, vexed with the filthy conversation of the wicked:** 8 **For that righteous man dwelling among them,** in **seeing** and **hearing, vexed his righteous soul** from day to day with **their unlawful deeds**..."

Just as He did in the days of both Noah and Lot, **God took all those that were faithful to Him** *(Rapture)* **before releasing His Judgment on the earth.** Unfortunately, man never learned from God's Judgment upon the people of Noah's days nor the judgment upon the people of Lot's days. **I do not have to tell you that the days before Rapture, modern man's wickedness and evil ways actually surpassed both the days of Noah and Lot!**

In western nations, Canada, USA and the United Nations, they **legislated and officially made the 'ways of Sodom' their** chosen lifestyle. **They took their wickedness further by demanding the right to kill babies in the womb even up to the day of birth!** They also, openly told God that they wanted nothing to do with Him as they removed all references to Him from schools, government and society as a whole. Always remember that the ungodly have **rejected God and do not want a society that operates on His principles.**

For example, satanic conventions, public worship of satan in national and international events became the order of the day for the 'enlightened western nations' while Christians watched in horror as events such as The Commonwealth Games, The Grammys and even the Super Bowl halftime performance became open satanic rituals. Therefore, as a **true Christian now, your soul will be very vexed** as Lot's was by the things you now **see and hear every day in your new world.** Be aware that **you are not alone** because it is **happening all over the new world and it will get worse before the Lord's Second Coming.**

Prepare for Betrayal from Those Around You

Many **Tribulation saints will experience** what the Lord said in **Mark 13:12:**

> "Now the **brother shall betray the brother to death,** and the **father the son; and children shall rise up against their parents, and shall cause them to be put to death.**"

According to the Lord, members of the same family will turn against their Christian relatives who chose to hold onto their faith in Christ and His Righteousness. Also, Children will turn their Christian parents into the authorities to be tortured and killed because of their parents' refusal to pledge their allegiance to the new world leader; the **antichrist.**

The Lord's Words began coming to pass even before Rapture occurred in nations where Christians were being persecuted. Know therefore that, if Christians were being persecuted before Rapture occurred, Christians **will be more**

<u>persecuted and killed</u> during the reign of the antichrist. **You must also be prepared for personal persecution from <u>your unbelieving family members</u>** and from your new society.

Many Will Renounce Christ

Many 'Christians' fell away before Rapture occurred so, do not be surprised to see many so-called **'Christians'** <u>renounce their faith in Christ</u> in the days after Rapture. Some will **take the Mark of the Beast or the name of the antichrist** *(I will talk about him later)* but **<u>you must be steadfast in your faith in Christ</u>**. We are told the following in **2 Thessalonians 2:1-5:**

> "Now we beseech you, brethren, by the coming of our Lord Jesus Christ, and by our gathering together unto him, 2 **That ye be not soon shaken in mind, or be troubled, neither by spirit, nor by word, nor by letter** as from us, as that the day of Christ is at hand.
>
> 3 **Let no man <u>deceive you</u> by any means: for that day shall not come, except there come <u>a falling away first</u>**, and that man of sin *(the antichrist)* be revealed, the son of perdition;
>
> 4 **Who opposeth and exalteth himself above all that is called God, or that is worshipped**; so that he as God sitteth in the temple of God, shewing himself that he is God. 5 Remember ye not, that, when I was yet with you, I told you these things?"

If people fell away before Rapture occurred, we know that some will also abandon their faith and follow the evil one because many will be deceived.

Man Became Prideful Due to Technology

Before Rapture occurred, the world tech leaders were very prideful that they can use technology to transform themselves and others; thereby making themselves gods. They forgot that even the technological accomplishments of man were from Almighty God. You must remember that God told us that in the last days, including the days before the Second Coming of Christ *(7 years after Rapture)* that man's knowledge will increase exponentially in **Daniel 12:4:**

> "But thou, O Daniel, shut up the words, and seal the book, even to the time of the end: many shall run to and fro, and **knowledge shall be increased**."

Just as the Word of God says, knowledge dramatically increased in the last days before Rapture but rather than give glory to God, man decided to play god by openly declaring that they can hack humans and control them so they can remake man to their liking.

They Believed They Were 'gods'

As such that they can control:

- Aging
- Death; man will live forever
- Create life; babies in the lab
- Control what man thinks, does or says
- Control man's movement
- Use of messenger ribonucleic acid *(MRNA)* technology to modify man's God-given DNA

They openly boasted of these abilities at their recent events of the World Economic Forum *(WEF)*. They rejoiced because the Covid-19 pandemic was an opportunity for them to implement many of their evil plans by weaponizing vaccine mandates, travel passports, more advanced global surveillance and cell phone tracking. God does not require any technology to know everything and see everything in order to judge them. Their destruction will be swift when the Lord comes back.

We are told in **1 Thessalonians 5:3** that sudden destruction shall come upon them:

> "For when they *(world leaders)* **shall say, Peace and Safety**; then **sudden destruction cometh upon them**, as travail upon a woman with child; and **they shall not escape**."

Chapter 4
The Beginning of God's Problem with Sin and Man

Sin as a Common Denominator

I want you to know that **sin is the 'common denominator'** or **'shared trait' of all the people that were left behind after Rapture.** This is why we must now address the **'problem of sin,'** because God's_ **impending judgment** is going to be **on sin and the sinner.** It is the whole reason why Rapture occurred to separate the **righteous** *(those who received the Lord Jesus as their Savior)* **from the sinner.** This is because from the beginning **God wants all men to live by His Word** — Luke: 4:4:

> "And Jesus answered him, saying, It is written, **That man shall not live by bread alone, but by every word of God.**"

This is the core of **God's desire for man and He wants every human being on earth** *(with no exception)* **to live by His Word that is written in the Bible.** The reason is because God knows that living by every Word that came out of His mouth will keep us away from the lies and deceptions of the devil which leads to sin. The end result of sin is death; eternal separation from God.

Definition of Sin

Sin is defined as the **disobedience or rebellion against God's spoken and written Word** in the Bible. **God Almighty hates sin** with a passion because, it is an **'Eternal Seed of Corruption'** that **begins the process of decay in a human Soul and body**. Nothing can stop this decaying process that eventually **results in death** and even after death, **it remains on the Soul** of the person. The corruption and decay of **sin defiles** and **contaminates** everything it touches and it **stinks**.

The **decaying effect of sin** is the reason why **we humans smell if we do not take a bath** and why we sweat, pee, poop, and our breath all stink. Over the years, humanity has tried to **mask the decaying stench of sin** with toothpastes, mouthwashes, perfumes, deodorants, air fresheners, cleaners, disinfectants and more. It is this <u>corruption that God wants to wash us free from</u> because He does not want it in Heaven.

Only God's Blood Can Remove Sin

Sin is a very serious problem because <u>nothing can remove its decaying process and stench but God's Own Blood</u>! This is why <u>God Himself had to come down to earth in His own Word</u> *(His Son Jesus)* <u>to shed His blood on the Cross</u> for the atonement or removal of our sins so that <u>He can renew our souls and at the end, give us new bodies.</u>

The scripture in **John 1:1-4** tells us that **Jesus Christ is the very Word that came out of God's** mouth and because **God creates with His Word**, the Lord Jesus created all things. **He is the vessel in which God came down to earth to save us from our sins:**

> "**In the beginning was <u>the Word</u>** *(Jesus)***, and the <u>Word was with God</u>, and <u>the Word was God</u>.** 2 The same was in the beginning with God. 3 **All things were made by him;** and without him was not anything made that was made. 4 **In him was <u>life</u>** *(God's life for all men)***; and the life was the light of men."**

Without coming down in His Word *(Jesus)* to **redeem or save us with <u>His own blood</u>, <u>God would have to judge all humanity and condemn us to eternal torment in hell for our sins</u>.** This is because without God's Blood through Christ, sin will leave humanity's spiritual **soul and body in a 'perpetual state of decay' like the 'living dead' for all eternity.**

After sacrificing His Son Jesus Christ on the Cross, God commanded everyone through Him to <u>repent of their sins</u> and <u>receive His atonement</u> so that <u>He can wash away our sins</u>. This is the only way that every human being can be reconciled back to God by His Son Jesus Christ. Meaning that, **believing in and receiving the Lord Jesus** *(God's Word)* is the **only available route for every human being to have their sins washed away** as we see in **John 3:16-18:**

> "For God so loved the world, that he gave <u>his</u> <u>only begotten Son,</u> that <u>whosoever believeth</u> <u>in him should not perish, but have everlasting</u> <u>life.</u> *17* For God sent not his Son into the world to condemn the world; **but that the world through him might be saved.** *18* <u>He that believeth on him</u> <u>is not condemned</u> *(doomed for hell):* <u>but he that</u> <u>believeth not is condemned already,</u> because he hath <u>not believed in the name of the only</u> <u>begotten Son of God."</u>

Think about it, it is like seeing someone drowning and you throw them a lifeline to save them. The same way, **God saw humanity drowning and dying from sin so, <u>He sent us</u> <u>His lifeline in Jesus Christ</u>.** Whoever <u>receives this lifeline</u> and <u>holds on to it, is saved</u> but <u>whoever does not</u> *(for whatever personal reason)* <u>accept the lifeline or drops it will die</u> in his or her sin. Again, <u>dying does not remove the sin but rather, the</u> <u>sin makes the person remain in a perpetual state of corruption.</u>

Christians Preaching for People to Receive Christ

As a result of the seriousness of sin for all humanity, **Christians have been <u>preaching</u> and <u>telling</u>** everyone for centuries to **<u>Repent</u>, <u>Believe</u>** and **<u>Receive</u> the Lord Jesus Christ so that they can be saved from their sins.** Many people have believed this message, made Jesus their Lord and have been walking faithfully with Him. Those who **believed, <u>made</u> <u>Jesus their Lord and Savior,</u> <u>had their sins washed away by</u> <u>the blood of Jesus</u>;** as long as they remained faithful to Him, He kept them safe.

Others <u>insisted</u> on holding on to **the religion of their families and some refused or rejected the message of salvation.** Therefore, at **Rapture, the Lord Jesus came, stood in the clouds, gave new bodies to those who were faithful to Him and took them out of the world. He left behind those** who <u>did not allow His blood to wash away their sins.</u> You see that, **God is not a 'respecter of persons;'** meaning that, **He does not play favorites.** He had to leave the 'unwashed in His blood' behind because, they carry the 'seed of corruption and decay' in their souls and as such are **stained, contaminated and defiled in God's sight.**

Jesus Christ is God's Only Answer to Sin

Until people <u>believe</u> the scripture in **John 3:16**, <u>repent of their sins</u> and <u>receive Jesus</u> as their Lord and Savior, even after Rapture, they cannot be saved but **when they come to Jesus Christ in faith and repentance, their sins will be washed away.** What this means to you is that, as long as you are alive, **it is <u>not too late</u> to make Jesus Christ your Lord and Savior.**

You must make this decision because, <u>**Jesus Christ is God's only answer or solution to the problem of sin in the world.**</u> The reason for this is as I stated before, **God Himself came down to earth in His Word** *(Jesus)* and <u>**reconciled all humanity to Himself on the Cross.**</u> What the Lord said in **John 14:6**, bears repeating here:

> "Jesus saith unto him, <u>**I am the way, the truth,**</u> and <u>**the life**</u>: <u>**no man cometh unto the Father, but by me.**</u>"

Apart from **the Lord Jesus Christ**, there is not a single person alive or who ever lived that **never sinned against God.** Therefore, everyone on earth needs to receive the Lord Jesus as their Lord so that His blood can reconcile them with God. This is why **making the Lord Jesus your Savior is a <u>big deal</u> to every man and woman who is alive right now; you must <u>take the time to really get to know Him</u>.** He alone can give God's Eternal Life to anyone who asks Him.

I say to you again that as a human being living on God's earth, you must <u>**believe and receive Christ as your Savoir or endure the consequences**</u> of rejecting Him by **facing God as <u>your Judge</u> instead of <u>your Heavenly Father</u>.** Anyone who dies and did not receive reconciliation with God through Christ, will have to personally answer to God for their sins since **they chose to hold on to their sins** and **rejected God's reconciliation in Christ.** No one is exempted from the need to be reconciled with God because, **God wants sin out of His perfect creation.**

No other Religion Has a Solution to Sin

It does not matter what religion you were born into; you must now turn and follow the Lord Jesus Christ to receive atonement for your sins. When you repent of your sins and ask Him for forgiveness, He will wash you with His Blood and give you eternal life; you will be reconciled with God. **No other religion can offer you this** because we are told in **Acts 4:12** that:

> "**Neither is there salvation in any other**: for **there is none other name** *(other than the name of Jesus)* **under heaven** given among men, **whereby we must be saved.**"

This is why no other religion can offer you a way out of sin because it is not there; they do not have it! The Jews offer the blood of goats and so do the Muslims at the end of Ramadan, but God said that the blood of goats and rams cannot take away human sin as we see in **Hebrews 10:4-7:**

> "**For it is not possible** that the **blood of bulls and of goats** should **take away sins.** *5* Wherefore when he *(Jesus)* cometh into the world, he saith, **Sacrifice and offering thou wouldest not** *(God does not like)*, **but a body hast thou prepared me** *(a human body to be sacrificed for sin)*: *6* **In burnt offerings and sacrifices for sin thou hast had no pleasure.** *7* Then said I, Lo, **I come (in the volume of the book it is written of me)** *(The Bible)*, **to do thy will, O God.**"

God's will was for the Lord Jesus to go to the Cross for us all as you just read from the scripture above. **God created a human body** to **house His Word;** His Son Jesus Christ so that **He can be sacrificed as the Lamb of God for our sin.** Again, **God's will**

was for the Lord Jesus to go to the Cross for all humanity and He did it gladly. Christ was more than willing to take our place on that Cross and to take the punishment for our sin.

Now, we will look at God's Creation of a perfect world and how it got contaminated by sin in the following subtitles.

God Created a Perfect World

When you read **God's Word** in **Genesis 1:1-31**, you will see how **God created the world and everything in it.** You will also see that **His finished product according to God's own standard** was **Very Good**; it was perfect because **God's works are always perfect!**

Note: I quoted the entire *Chapter One* of the *Book of Genesis* below so that those **who practice other religions and have never read about how the God of the Bible created the world and everything in it can read it here:**

"**In the beginning God created the heaven and the earth.** 2 And the earth was without form, and void; and darkness was upon the face of the deep. And the Spirit of God moved upon the face of the waters. 3 **And God said, Let there be light: and there was light.** 4 **And God saw the light, that it was good:** and **God divided the light from the darkness.**

5 And **God called the light Day**, and the **darkness he called Night.** And the evening and the morning were the first day. 6 And God said, **Let there be a firmament in the midst of the waters, and let it divide the waters from the waters.** 7 And God made the firmament, and divided the waters which were under the firmament from the waters which were above the firmament: and it was so.

8 And **God called the firmament Heaven.** And the evening and the morning were the second day. 9 And **God said, Let the waters under the heaven be gathered together unto one place, and let the dry**

land appear: and it was so. 10 And **God called the dry land Earth**; and **the gathering together of the waters called he Seas**: and **God saw that it was good.**

11 And **God said, Let the earth bring forth grass, the herb yielding seed, and the fruit tree yielding fruit after his kind, whose seed is in itself, upon the earth**: and it was so. 12 And the earth brought forth grass, and herb yielding seed after his kind, and the tree yielding fruit, whose seed was in itself, after his kind: and **God saw that it was good.** 13 And the evening and the morning were the third day.

14 And **God said, Let there be lights in the firmament of the heaven to divide the day from the night; and let them be for signs, and for seasons, and for days, and years:** 15 And let them be for lights in the firmament of the heaven to give light upon the earth: and it was so. 16 And **God made two great lights; the greater light to rule the day, and the lesser light to rule the night: he made the stars also.**

17 And God set them in the firmament of the heaven to give light upon the earth, 18 And **to rule over the day and over the night, and to divide the light from the darkness: and God saw that it was good.** 19 And the evening and the morning were the fourth day. 20 And **God said, Let the waters bring forth abundantly the moving creature that hath life, and fowl that may fly above the earth in the open firmament of heaven.**

21 And **God created great whales, and every living creature that moveth, which the waters brought forth abundantly, after their kind, and every winged fowl after his kind: and God saw that it was good.** 22 And God blessed them, saying, Be fruitful, and multiply, and fill the waters in the seas, and let fowl multiply in the earth. 23 And the evening and the morning were the fifth day.

24 And **God said, Let the earth bring forth the living creature after his kind, cattle, and creeping thing, and beast of the earth after his kind:** and it was so. 25 And **God made the beast of the earth after his kind, and cattle after their kind, and everything that creepeth upon the earth after his kind:** and **God saw that it was good.** 26 And **God said, Let us make man** (*Adam*) **in our image, after our likeness:** and **let them have dominion over** the fish of the sea, and over the fowl of the air, and over the cattle, and over all the earth, and over every creeping thing that creepeth upon the earth.

27 So **God created man in his own image, in the image of God created he him; male and female created he them** (*All those who are confused about their God-assigned gender should see this*). 28 **And God blessed them, and God said unto them, Be fruitful, and multiply, and replenish the earth** (*All those who are concerned about over-population of man on earth should read this*), and subdue it: and have dominion over the fish of the sea, and over the fowl of the air, and over every living thing that moveth upon the earth.

29 And God said, Behold, I have given you every herb bearing seed, which is upon the face of all the earth, and every tree, in the which is the fruit of a tree yielding seed; **to you it shall be for meat.** 30 And to every beast of the earth, and to every fowl of the air, and to everything that creepeth upon the earth, wherein there is life, I have given every green herb for meat: and it was so. 31 **And God saw everything that he had made**, and, behold, **it was very good.** And the evening and the morning were the sixth day."

As you read in Genesis, God's finished work of creation was, "**very good.**" The question is: **How did sin** (*evil*) **enter into God's Creation?**

How Sin Entered God's Perfect Creation

The answer to the question: <u>how did sin enter into God's perfect creation</u> is <u>Lucifer</u>. You have been reading about God's **'Problem with Sin'** in humanity but now you will see, the **'Origin of Sin'** and its <u>devastating consequences</u> on **God's Creation**. It all began with **'a rebellious Cherub;'** formerly called **Lucifer**. The Cherubim carry the Glory of God and they wait upon Him continually but Lucifer was created as one of the higher Cherubs with a unique assignment.

Lucifer's God-given Assignment

He was one of **God's highest** and **strongest Cherubs** and his name **Lucifer**, means **light**. God created him to be very beautiful and decked him with **every precious stone** *(they are listed in the scripture below)*; <u>his vocal cords</u> were a built-in <u>musical pipe organ</u> for great **angelic singing** that could be heard in all the sanctuaries that God gave him charge over. In fact, God placed Lucifer in charge of the **first beings** that were **on earth** *(not human beings of today)*, and in **other planets.**

His job was to <u>teach these beings about who God is</u>, show them **God's goodness** and to lead them in **praise and worship of God Almighty**; he was their God-assigned covering like a **pastor**. These beings were on earth and other planets where they had **sanctuaries or <u>congregations to worship God Almighty</u>** and Lucifer was their worship leader. For this reason, God made him with **precious stones,** gave him <u>vocal cords made as a musical organ</u> and <u>endowed him with great beauty</u> so that <u>during praise and worship,</u> Lucifer <u>will light-up</u> and the precious stones on him became a spectacular display of beauty before these beings!

They would become enamored by the **display of his beauty** and <u>at the awesomeness of the God who gave him such beauty</u>. After a long while, Lucifer became **filled with pride and jealousy** of **God Almighty** and <u>it resulted in his self-conceived evil</u>; **sin.** The nature of this sin is first revealed to us by what God said to Lucifer in **Ezekiel 28:13-19:**

"Thou *(Lucifer)* hast been in Eden the garden of God; **every precious stone was thy covering,** the **sardius, topaz,** and the **diamond,** the **beryl,** the **onyx,** and the **jasper,** the **sapphire,** the **emerald,** and the **carbuncle,** and **gold:** the **workmanship of thy tabrets and of thy pipes** *(vocal cords)* was prepared in thee **in the day that thou wast created.**

14 Thou art the **anointed cherub that covereth** *(like a pastor)*; **and I have set thee so:** thou wast upon the holy mountain of God; thou **hast walked up and down in the midst of the stones of fire** *(the Place of God's power)* 15 **Thou wast perfect in thy ways from the day that thou wast created, till iniquity** *(self-will)* **was found in thee.**

16 By the **multitude of thy merchandise** *(self-promoting as worthy of worship)* **they have filled the midst of thee with violence,** and **thou hast Sinned:** therefore **I will cast thee as profane out of the mountain of God:** and **I will destroy thee, O covering cherub, from the midst of the stones of fire** *(position of power).* 17 **Thine heart was lifted up** *(pride)* **because of thy beauty, thou hast corrupted thy wisdom** *(as a self-promoter, he began to corrupt the Word of God)* by reason of thy brightness: I will cast thee to the ground, I will lay thee before kings, that they may behold thee.

18 **Thou hast defiled thy Sanctuaries by the multitude of thine iniquities** *(he taught the beings under him blasphemy against God),* **by the iniquity of thy traffick** *(selling himself as a counterfeit of God);* therefore will I bring forth a fire from the midst of thee, it shall devour thee, and **I will bring thee to ashes upon the earth in the sight of all them that behold thee.** 19 **All they that know thee among the people shall be astonished at thee** *(human beings never saw Lucifer as he was before his sin but the*

first beings on earth did): **thou shalt be a terror, and never shalt thou be any more.**"

As you just read from God's Word above, Lucifer began to **covet God's Position** (*the Most High God*), and in his deluded mind **wanted** to be **worshipped** just as God was being worshipped. **This is why to this day he loves to receive worship from those practicing idolatry** (*pagan religions*); **he is the inventor of it!** It was the **pride, lust, envy,** and **covetousness** that Lucifer had for **God's Position and Power** that made him **desire to be like the Most High God so that he can also receive worship**.

This is how **Lucifer** introduced **rebellion** and an **evil desire** (*sin*) **into God's perfect creation.** He single handedly **conceived an evil desire** and **brought forth sin**! Again, we see the report of this **Luciferian sin that was rooted in pride, lust, envy, jealousy, and covetousness** recorded in **Isaiah 14:12-15**:

> "**How art thou fallen from heaven, O Lucifer,** son of the morning! how art thou cut down to the ground, which didst weaken the nations! 13 **For thou hast said in thine heart, I will ascend into heaven, I will exalt my throne above the stars of God** (*God's angels*):
>
> **I will sit also** (*a statement of lust and covetousness*) **upon the mount of the congregation** (*the beings who congregate to worship God on earth and other planets*) **in the sides of the north** (*where God sits*): 14 **I will ascend above the heights of the clouds; I will be like the Most High** (*a statement of pride, lust and covetousness*). 15 Yet thou shalt **be brought down to hell,** to the sides of the pit."

After he **corrupted all the beings** (*sanctuaries or congregations*) that God gave him charge over, **Lucifer** also, **drew a third of God's angels** that were **under his command into his rebellion against God.** In response, **God abased, degraded,**

belittled and **demoted** him to the **status of a devil**; meaning, <u>one only fit to be trodden under foot</u>! A carcass to be thrown into the fire of hell and later into the Lake of Fire!

Unfortunately, the **non-human beings** that were on earth that he **taught rebellion and blasphemy against God** *(his former congregations)*, are <u>now the demons</u> or <u>evil spirits</u> that **humanity wrestles with every day.** The <u>fallen angels</u> are now <u>the principalities</u> or **wicked spirits <u>over nations</u> and <u>world leaders.</u>** They inspire people and world leaders to promote and make ungodly laws as well as to be self-seeking in their agenda. Also, all the planets Lucifer was in charge of became desolate when God in His anger overthrew him and made the planets desolate to this day. God restored only the earth for man *(Adam)* to dwell in. This is why there is no alien life (UFOs) on other planets. They are still desolate with no life but demons deceive people by pretending to be aliens from other planets.

All the devil's actions confirmed what the Lord Jesus said in **Matthew 7:18-20:**

> "<u>A good tree cannot bring forth evil fruit</u>, **neither can a <u>corrupt tree bring forth good fruit</u>** *(the devil is a corrupt Tree).* 19 Every tree that bringeth not forth good fruit is hewn down, and cast into the fire. 20 **Wherefore by their fruits ye shall know them.**"

Again, because of the <u>**devil's corrupt nature and contaminating actions**</u>, he is only fit for the Lake of Fire.

Understanding Sin and its Nature

Sin is actually a spirit; the disobedient spirit and prideful nature of the devil and it always results in death. As we saw in Lucifer; <u>now called the devil,</u> sin is <u>capable of conceiving and giving birth</u> as a pregnant woman does which is exactly what Lucifer did all by himself because of **his lust for God's power and position.** The **devil is a <u>corrupt tree</u>** and lust is his primary tool of entrapping people, but know that any man or woman who operates in his lustful ways can only expect death as we are warned in **James 1:14-15:**

> **"But every man is tempted, when he is drawn away of his own lust, and enticed**. 15 Then when lust hath conceived, <u>it bringeth forth sin</u>: and **sin, when it is finished, <u>bringeth forth death</u>."**

Lust is the **ungodly inspiration** from the devil to walk in **pride, envy, covetousness, and jealousy** but the end result of **lust is sin** which violates God's Word. **Any action that violates God's Word is sin while death is being eternally separated from God** in hell. What James is saying in the above scripture is that <u>lust is the root of sin and the tool the devil uses as a</u> <u>bait</u>. We see this in the devil's dealings with Adam and Eve.

God's Commandment to Adam

When God created **Adam** *(the first man from whom humanity descended)*, **He gave him His own Breath** *(spirit)* and a **<u>free will</u>** but with a **commandment to choose only <u>good</u> and stay away from <u>evil</u>** which were **both represented as Trees** in the Garden of Eden. God also gave **Adam authority** to rule over all the earth. God specifically told Adam that **the day he tastes evil, he shall <u>surely die</u>** — Genesis 2:8-23:

> **"And the LORD God formed man of the dust of the ground, and breathed into his nostrils the breath of life;** and **man became a living soul** *(alive to God forever)*. 8 And **the LORD God planted a garden** eastward in Eden; and **there he put the man whom he had formed**. 9 And out of the ground made the LORD God to grow every tree that is pleasant to the sight, and good for food; the **<u>tree of life</u>** *(Jesus)* also in the midst of the garden, and the **<u>tree of knowledge of good and evil</u>** *(the devil, his lies and deceptions)*...
>
> 15 And the LORD God took the man, and put him into the garden of Eden to dress it and **to keep it**

(Govern it). 16 **And the LORD God commanded the man**, saying, **of every tree of the garden thou mayest freely eat**: 17 **But of the tree of the knowledge of good and evil** *(the fruit is the devil's counsel),* **thou shalt not eat of it**: for in the day that **thou eatest thereof thou shalt surely die** *(spiritually and physically).* 18 And the LORD God said, It is not good that the man should be alone; I will make him an help meet for him *(give him a wife)...*

21 And the LORD God caused a deep sleep to fall upon Adam, and he slept: and he took one of his ribs, and closed up the flesh instead thereof; 22 And **the rib, which the LORD God had taken from man, made he a woman, and brought her unto the man.** 23 And Adam said, This is now bone of my bones, and flesh of my flesh: **she shall be called Woman** *(Eve),* because **she was taken out of Man."**

How the Devil Got Eve and Adam to Desire Evil

In the scripture below, you will clearly see how **lust was the bait the devil used to make Eve desire to experience or taste evil**. This **lust for the taste of evil** and **disobedience of God's Word to stay away from evil** is known as man's 'Original Sin' in the **Garden of Eden**. As a result of **tasting evil for all mankind, all of humanity has experienced the destructive and wickedness of evil**. Every human being can now wonder, **how a person in their right mind will ever desire to experience evil** in his or her life! Yet, this is what Eve ignorantly desired and Adam of his own free will chose for himself and for all humanity.

What happened to **Eve** in the Garden of Eden, shows us the **power of lust** and the **damage it does** because **there is not a human being alive** that has not experienced a part of the **devastations of evil** through **wars, famines, earthquakes,** plagues, sicknesses, diseases, murders, rapes, pre-mature death in the family, loss, theft, evil acts, man's inhumanity to man, etc.

Unfortunately, **once evil** *(sin)* **was brought into** the **Human Soul**, it became an 'Eternal Seed of Corruption and Decay' that **nothing can remove but God's own blood**. Evil in a human soul is like **an Apple that begins to <u>rot in its core</u> and <u>nothing can stop the process till it all rots</u>**. Remember, this is the history of man's beginning and his walk with God as recorded in **Genesis 3:1-7:**

> "Now the **serpent** *(devil)* was more **subtil** *(conniving)* than any beast of the field which the LORD God had made. And **he said unto the woman** *(Eve)*, Yea, **hath God said, Ye shall not eat of every tree of the garden?** 2 And the woman said unto the serpent, **We may eat of the fruit of the trees of the garden:**
>
> 3 **But of the fruit of the tree which is in the midst of the garden, God hath said, Ye shall not eat of it, neither shall ye touch it, <u>lest ye die.</u>** 4 And **the serpent said unto the woman** *(Eve)*, **Ye shall not surely die:** 5 For God doth know that in the day ye eat thereof, then **your eyes shall be opened**, and ye **shall be as gods**, knowing **good** and **evil.**
>
> 6 And when the **woman saw** *(lust)* that **the tree was good for food,** and that it was **pleasant to the eyes** *(still lust)*, and a tree **to be desired to make one wise** *(lustful desire)*, she took of the fruit thereof, and **did eat**, and **gave also unto her husband with her; and he did eat.** 7 And the eyes of them both were opened, and they knew that they were naked *(lacking God's covering protection)*; and they sewed fig leaves together, and made themselves aprons."

Adam and Eve not only disobeyed God's commandment, but they were **unrepentant**; which is **the nature of the devil** that he immediately gave them. As you will see below, when **God confronted them** about their sin, they both **made excuses**. Instead of **repenting and asking God for forgiveness**, they played the 'Blame Game' with God. Eve blamed the serpent and Adam blamed both God and Eve as we see in **Genesis 3:10-13:**

> "And he said, I heard thy voice in the garden, and I was afraid, because I was naked; and I hid myself. *11* And he *(God)* said, Who told thee that thou wast naked? **Hast thou eaten of the tree, whereof I commanded thee that thou shouldest not eat?**
> *12* And the man said, **The woman whom thou gavest to be with me, she gave me of the tree, and I did eat.** *13* **And the LORD God said unto the woman, What is this that thou hast done?** And the woman said, **The serpent beguiled me, and I did eat.**"

As you just read, **God gave them the opportunity to repent and ask for forgiveness in the way He posed His question to them**, but it was very sad that they were **unrepentant** because again, **the nature of the devil was already working in them.**

Beginning of the Generations of Sinners

By obeying the serpent *(the devil)* rather than obeying God, Adam and Eve chose not to live by the Word of God but by the word *(lies)* of the devil. In so doing, they rebelled against God and **they unleashed sin on all their descendants** *(all of humanity)*! **This is how every human being through Adam acquired the lying, wicked and evil nature of the devil.** In other words, because of their actions, the whole world has been wrestling with sin and its evils even to this day.

Adam and Eve's rebellion was carried to a higher level by their son **Cain** who knew that **God required a blood sacrifice** *(a lamb)* but **willfully** brought God a **grain sacrifice**; an act of iniquity *(self-will)*. **God rejected his sacrifice but accepted that of Abel,** his brother as recorded in **Genesis 4:1-8**:

> "And **Adam knew Eve his wife;** and **she conceived, and bare Cain**, and said, I have gotten a man from the LORD. 2 And **she again bare his brother Abel**. And **Abel was a keeper of sheep, but Cain was a tiller of the ground.** 3 And in process of time it came to pass, that **Cain brought of the fruit of the ground** an offering unto the LORD.
>
> 4 **And Abel, he also brought of the firstlings of his flock and of the fat thereof.** And the LORD had respect unto Abel and to his offering: 5 But unto Cain and to his offering he had not respect. And Cain was very wroth, and his countenance fell. 6 **And the LORD said unto Cain, Why art thou wroth? and why is thy countenance fallen?**
>
> 7 **If thou doest well, shalt thou not be accepted? and if thou doest not well, sin** *(the devil)* **lieth at the door. And unto thee shall be his desire, and thou shalt rule over him.** 8 And Cain talked with Abel his brother: and it came to pass, when they were in the field, **that Cain rose up against Abel his brother, and slew him.**"

Cain chose to ignore God's Word that sin was lying at the door of his disobedience and that **sin's desire** is to **have dominion over him**. Instead of correcting his actions as God instructed him, **Cain chose not to take God's counsel** but to align his actions with the **devil** *(sin)* **that was waiting for him at the door of disobedience.** His response was to **kill his brother Abel who was living according to God's Word.** Just like Cain, sin is always at the door of all those who choose not to listen to God's Word.

This is the **hidden truth** about the **mystery of the working of sin** that **most people do not know in their walk with**

the Lord. They are not aware that **sin is always waiting at the door for anyone who chooses to disregard or disobey the Word of God.** Once sin gets hold of a person at the door of disobedience to God's Word, **it can then lead the person to do many other things that are ungodly and more sinful!** Can you imagine it, there were only two brothers on earth with their parents and one killed the other? **The wickedness of sin has been multiplying since Adam and Eve unleashed it on the world.**

God in His mercy gave Adam and Eve another son called **Seth** because Cain had chosen to follow the devil. We know that Seth and his descendants also wrestled with sin because they were among the first people to be directly impacted by Adam and Eve's open door to sin. Just as the door of sin was opened against **Seth and his descendants, the door of sin remains wide-open against us** though thousands of generations have passed since Adam and Eve.

We All Contributed Our Share to the Sins of the World

Every one of us has **added our own personal sins to this 'original sin' that we all inherited** from Adam and Eve. We all chose to live our lives on our own terms and do things our way *(iniquity)* **without obeying God's Word in the Bible;** meaning that we lived in **rebellion** against God. This is why God concluded all of us to be in sin as we read in **Romans 3:9-12:**

> "...For we have before proved **both Jews** and **Gentiles,** that **they are all under sin;** *10* As it is written, **There is none righteous, no, not one:** *11* **There is none that understandeth, there is none that seeketh after God.**
>
> *12* They are all gone out of the way, **they are together become unprofitable** *(useless to God);* **there is none that doeth good, no, not one.**"

As you can see, none of us *(every human being)* was righteous before God. To receive God's righteousness, you must respond to **God's gift of salvation in His Son** by **believing** that **Jesus Christ is the Son of God;** some **people have a problem** with this concept. I say to you assuredly that, <u>God cannot save you if you refuse to believe that Jesus Christ is the Son of God.</u>

Therefore, you must believe that as **the Son of God, He died on the Cross for your sins** and **that on the third day, God the Father raised Him up** from **the dead to give you eternal life.** Although you are still living in this world after your salvation, **you are not to go back to being a servant of sin but to resist sin and its lusts.**

As I stated before, what people do not understand is that according to the scriptures, **sin has the ability to conceive and bring forth death** in **those who let it into their lives.** I reiterate what was written in **James 1:14-15** here:

> "But **every man is tempted** (*just as Eve and many people*), when he is drawn away of his **own lust, and enticed.** *15* Then **when lust hath conceived,** it bringeth forth sin: and **sin, when it is finished, bringeth forth death** (*eternal separation from God in hell*)."

Also, **sin seeks to <u>hold people in captivity</u> or dominate them** throughout their lifetime. **The devil seeks to make people live all their lives in sin.** This is why those who follow the Lord Jesus are told in **Romans 6:6-14** not to serve sin and not to let sin have dominion over them:

> "**Knowing this, that <u>our old man</u>** (*who we were before being Born Again in Christ*) **is crucified with him, that <u>the body of sin might be destroyed</u>, that henceforth we should not serve sin.** *7* **For he that is dead is freed from sin** (*crucified with Christ spiritually*). *8* **<u>Now if we be dead with Christ, we believe that we shall also live with him</u>**:
>
> *9* Knowing that Christ being raised from the dead dieth no more; death hath no more dominion over him. *10* For in that he died, he died unto sin once: but in that he liveth, he liveth unto God. *11*

Likewise <u>reckon ye also yourselves to be dead indeed unto sin,</u> but <u>alive unto God through Jesus Christ our Lord</u>.

12 **Let not sin therefore reign in your mortal body, that ye should obey it in the lusts thereof.** 13 <u>**Neither yield ye your members as instruments of unrighteousness unto sin**</u>: but yield yourselves unto God, as those that are alive from the dead, and your members as instruments of righteousness unto God. 14 <u>**For sin shall not have dominion over you**</u>: for ye are not under the law, <u>**but under grace**</u>."

Chapter 5
Why God Sent the Lord Jesus into the World

God's Judgment on Humanity because of Sin

We were all **under God's judgment because of our sins** until **the Lord Jesus went to the Cross for us**. This is why **Romans 3:23** says:

> "For **all have sinned**, and come short of the glory of God *(God's protection)* ..."

The above statement applies to every human being that has ever lived on earth **except Jesus Christ who had no sin**. In **Ezekiel 18:4**, we see **God's Death Sentence** on all humanity:

> "Behold, **all souls are mine**; as the soul of the father, so also the soul of the son is mine: **the soul that sinneth, it shall die.**"

Again, it was **either God condemn us all to hell or find a way to save us.** He made a way for us by sending His Son Jesus Christ to the Cross for us all and He **paid the full price** that God required from us all because of our sins. I reiterate that **the Lord Jesus Christ paid the 'Death Penalty' that God imposed on us all because of our sins.**

Animals and the Earth Were Defiled by Sin

From all that you have read in the previous chapter, you can see that God has been dealing with the '**Problem of Sin**' in man **ever since man tasted evil** in the Garden of Eden. **God hates sin and does not want it near Him** or in His creation because as you have personally experienced, **it has a very destructive nature**. It defiled God's perfect creation of both man, **animals** *(who did not have a violent nature before)* as well as the Earth itself!

When Adam rebelled against God, everything on earth that Adam was Lord over in return, rebelled against him.

Animals turned against man because Adam's contamination also affected them; **even the earth became contaminated with sin when it received Abel's blood** *(the first human blood)* **shed on earth by Cain** his brother. This is why as I will discuss later, the earth itself will be cleansed by the blood of Jesus. God will restore it by renovating it.

The Lord Jesus Christ Came to Save the World

To understand why Christ came into the world, you have to begin with the **ministry of John the Baptist** because, John the Baptist was **sent by God the Father** to baptize people with water in preparation for the revelation of the Messiah *(Jesus Christ)* who will **be <u>the one to baptize them with the Holy Spirit</u>.** Therefore, **John** as the 'Forerunner' of the Messiah, was also to **announce the Lord Jesus Christ <u>as the Lamb of God born to be slayed in order to take away the sin of the world</u>** — John 1:29:

> "The next day **John seeth Jesus coming unto him**, and saith, **Behold the Lamb of God, which taketh away the sin of the world**."

From John statement's, we can see that one of the reasons why the Lord came into the world was to take away the sin of the world. If you noticed, the scripture says, "**the Sin of the World**." The reason for using **sin in a singular term** is because **<u>the world only has one sin against God</u>**.

This is why **John did not say the sins of the world** but the **sin of the world.** Your question at this time should be: **<u>What is the sin of the world?</u>** The answer is **<u>Rebellion</u>** or **disobedience of God's Word** —**this is the sin of the world** that began with Adam and Eve in the Garden of Eden. This is why the Lord Jesus came into the world as **God's Lamb to be sacrificed for the sin of all humanity** as was announced by John the Baptist and **accomplished by the Lord Jesus on the Cross.**

As we already saw in scripture, '**Man's Original Sin**' <u>**took place the day**</u> that Adam and Eve chose to obey the devil's words instead of the Word of God. Since then, every human being came under God's judgment of condemnation for disobeying His Words or commandments. Not just the **Jews** but the **Gentiles** (*the rest of the world*) came **under God's condemnation** for their disobedience of God's **Law of Conscience**.

Although God did not write His laws on tablets for the Gentiles as He did for the Jews, He wrote His laws of right and wrong on every human conscience. This is why we are told in **Romans 2:12-16** that the conscience of the **Gentiles serves as their law**:

> "For as many as have sinned without law shall also perish without law: and as many as have sinned in the law shall be judged by the law; 13 For not the hearers of the law are just before God, but the doers of the law shall be justified. 14 For when the Gentiles, which have not the law, do by nature the things contained in the law, these, having not the law, are a law unto themselves:

> 15 Which shew the work of the law written in their hearts, their conscience also bearing witness, and their thoughts the mean while accusing or else excusing one another 16 In the day when God shall judge the secrets of men by Jesus Christ according to my gospel."

We and all the generations before us came **under God's curse because of our sins** as we are told in **Proverbs 26:2** that a curse will not happen unless a person has earned it (*meaning you sinned*):

> "As the bird by wandering, as the swallow by flying, so the curse causeless shall not come."

This is why we have generational curses that we call family curses. A good example of this is a person who is a rapist. All his or her **descendants will be under the curse of rape**. As a result, **there will always be an incident of rape that occurs in his or her family because the seed of rape was sown by the rapist.** The Lord came to take away all the curses that were on humanity. **It is one of the reasons that God the Father sacrificed His Son** as we see in — Isaiah 53:8-10:

> "...For he *(Jesus)* **was cut off out of the land of the living** *(killed)*: **for the transgression** *(sin)* **of my people was he stricken.** *9* And he made his grave with the wicked, and with the rich in his death; because he had done no violence, neither was any deceit in his mouth. *10* **Yet it pleased the LORD to bruise him; he hath put him to grief:** **when thou shalt make his soul an offering for sin**..."

Every Human Being Must Answer: Who is Jesus Christ?

After years of walking with Him, the Lord Jesus wanted His disciples to **answer the question of who they believe or say that He is.** He asked them this question in **Matthew 16:15**:

> "He saith unto them, **But whom say ye that I am?**"

The disciple named **Simon Peter answered** and said in **Matthew 16:16**:

> "...Thou art the Christ, **the Son of the living God.**"

The **Lord Jesus** then told us that it is God the Father that gives us *(as He did Simon),* **the revelation knowledge of who He is** — Matthew 16:17:

> "And Jesus answered and said unto him, Blessed art thou, Simon Barjona: for **flesh and blood** *(human Knowledge)* **hath not revealed it unto thee, but my Father which is in heaven.**"

Besides His disciple, the **Lord Jesus wants every adult human** being to also answer the question of **who they say He is** — Matthew 16:13-15:

> "... **Whom do men** *(humanity)* **say that I the Son of man am?** *14* And they said, Some say that thou art

John the Baptist: some, Elias; and others, Jeremias, or one of the prophets. *15* He saith unto them, **But whom say ye that I am?**"

I want you to know that your answer to this question **will determine the fate of your Soul for all eternity.** Due to the importance of your answer to this question, **you cannot afford to dismiss, ignore, reject it or come up with your own opinion about Jesus Christ** without taking the time find out from the Bible, who He really is.

The Lord Jesus Christ Himself **needs you to also answer the question of who He is to you and why He came into this world.** This is because, if you ever hope to be with God in Heaven at the end of your life, **you must know that the Lord Jesus Christ is the Son of God who came as God's Lamb to take away the sin of the world. Any other answer will deny you access into Heaven** because again, this is what the Lord Jesus said about who He is in **John 14:6:**

> "Jesus saith unto him, **I Am** the **Way,** the **Truth,** and **the Life: No Man cometh unto the Father** (*God*), **but By Me.**"

He is the Key to Heaven; meaning, the only Way that God the Father provided for all humanity to get to Him because the **Lord Jesus is the Word of God** (*the Truth*) **tabernacled or dwelling in a human body!** He alone can give us God's Life which is the life that can live in Heaven and the New Earth under His reign. No one can get around Him to get to God as revealed in **Acts 4:12:**

> "**Neither is there salvation in any other: for there is none other name under heaven** given among men, **whereby we must be saved.**"

Again, know that the Lord Jesus is the only way for you to get to God. You cannot find a way in any other religion. Your choice: it is either the Lord Jesus or hell. Do you now see why your answer to the question of **who is Jesus, is very critical** to the eternal destination of your Soul? Do you also see why **the wrong answer** to the question of who **Jesus Christ is, will put you in hell forever?** For one thing, Rapture has already happened and you missed it and He is giving you a second chance to come to Him for the Salvation of your soul.

The Answer to Why We are Here on Earth

If you have ever wondered why we humans are here on earth or what the purpose of life is, here is your answer from God Almighty. We all were once alive to God in Adam but when Adam sinned against God, we all died spiritually; meaning that we became separated from God. **None of us had any say when Adam made the choice to taste evil for us that resulted in our spiritual death.**

Therefore, God sends every one of us to earth so that we can choose whether or not we want to be made Alive to Him; to choose Life instead of the Death that Adam chose for us. **The whole purpose of our being on earth** is not to make money, become politically and financially powerful, get famous, and acquire material possessions **but to be made Alive to God in Christ Jesus**.

It is the reason that acquiring things do not satisfy the human soul. The more you acquire things, the more dissatisfied and thirsty your soul gets because only the Life of God can satisfy it and you can only get this Life by believing in Christ. **Therefore, know that you are here on earth to choose whether or not you want to return to God; to be Alive with God in Christ or remain under the devil.**

We All Need Salvation

We are given the **biblical definition of Salvation** in **Romans 10:8-11:**

> "But what saith it? The **word is nigh thee, even in thy mouth,** and **in thy heart**: that is, **the word of faith, which we preach;** 9 **That if thou shalt confess with thy mouth the Lord Jesus, and shalt**

believe in thine heart that God hath raised him from the dead, thou shalt be saved.

10 For **with the heart man believeth unto righteous-ness; and with the mouth confession is made unto salvation**. *11* For the scripture saith, **Whosoever believeth on him shall not be ashamed**."

Salvation means being delivered or spared by God from His own wrath to be poured out on all sinners and **being reconciled with Him by the washing away of our sins with the Blood of Jesus Christ**. Being brought by Christ to God the Father as just or justified by His blood that washed away your sins. It means that **you can stand before the Most Holy God blameless** — Colossians 1:22:

"In the body of his flesh through death, **to present you** *(to God the Father as)* **holy** and **unblameable** and **unreproveable in his sight**."

When Christ has accomplished all that concerns our salvation, **He is going to present all Believers to His Father** and **we will all be without the stain or wrinkle of sin** and **will be blameless of all our sins** because **He washed us in His own blood!**

"That **he might present it to himself** *(Christ and the Father are one)* **a glorious** Church *(Believers)*, not having spot, or wrinkle, or any such thing; but that **it should be holy** and **without blemish**" (Ephesians 5:27).

Only 'Incorruptible New Human Bodies' Can Live in Heaven

God has no room for corrupted, decaying souls and bodies in His Heaven. This is why all who enter are those that have been washed clean by the blood of Jesus Christ. A person with a mind and a body corrupted by sin cannot enter Heaven because they cannot withstand the glory of God while in their decaying bodies. **Since no corruption is allowed in Heaven,** there is no need for **bathrooms** and **toilets** there.

Also, **anyone with a non-regenerated mind, body and soul cannot be allowed into Heaven** because there is **no place for decay and stench there.** Yes, those in Heaven do not sweat from decay, they do not poop and they do not emit foul odors. Therefore, those who **did not belong to the Lord Jesus, deprived themselves of the only opportunity in Christ to have God cleanse them, renew their minds** *(conscience)*, **and give them new bodies that can live in Heaven.**

This is the reason we are told that those who are still in their corruptible body of flesh and blood cannot inherit the Kingdom of God. As a result, **all those who were 'caught–up' at Rapture, had their bodies changed into new bodies** as they were being taken — **1 Corinthians 15:50-55:**

> "Now this I say, brethren, that **flesh and blood cannot inherit the kingdom of God;** neither doth corruption inherit incorruption. *51* **Behold, I shew you a mystery; We shall not all sleep, but we shall all be changed,** *52* **In a moment, in the twinkling of an eye, at the last trump: for the trumpet shall sound, and the dead shall be raised incorruptible, and we shall be changed**

> *53* **For this corruptible** *(bodies)* **must put on incorruption, and this mortal must put on immortality.** *54* So when this corruptible shall have put on incorruption, and this mortal shall have put on immortality, then shall be brought to pass the saying that is written, Death is swallowed up in victory. *55* O death, where is thy sting? O grave, where is thy victory?"

Therefore, all those **who are rejecting Christ are essentially rejecting Heaven and the** only way **to get into it. They are depriving God of the only opportunity to wipe away their tears, sorrows, sufferings, <u>cleanse their souls from the consciousness of sin and its wickedness and to receive new bodies</u>!**

As a result, when they are in hell, **they will forever be conscious of the wickedness and the ungodly lives they lived on earth with the full awareness that they deserved to be in hell. They will live their eternity in regrets with no absolution.** As a matter of fact, everyone in hell can tell you all the wickedness that placed them in hell because they can never forget them.

Importance of the Message of Salvation

Again, we all sinned in Adam and came under **God's judgment of death** but, God's Word in **Romans 6:23** tells us that **we can escape the judgment of death and receive God's Gift of Eternal Life when we receive Christ as our Lord:**

> "**For the wages of sin is death**, but the **gift of God is Eternal Life in Christ Jesus our Lord**."

Christ is the only one who has never sinned; <u>we have all sinned against God and need His forgiveness</u> so that at the end of our lives, He does not condemn us to hell. This is why you must now be ready to receive His Salvation so that **<u>you do not miss Eternal Life</u> this time around.** I say to you again that, that **<u>the Lord Jesus made provisions for people to come to Him even after Rapture has occurred.</u>**

Therefore, **you will hear of people making Jesus Christ their Savior and trusting Him to see them through these rough times.** You should be one of them because **without the salvation that God gave humanity through the Lord Jesus Christ, there is no hope for any human being.**

There Can be No Salvation without Repentance

God's definition of Repentance is in Ezekiel 14:6 as follows:

> "...Thus saith the Lord GOD; **Repent, and <u>turn yourselves from your idols</u>; and <u>turn away your faces from all your abominations</u>**."

And in **Ezekiel 33:11** God said:

> "Say unto them, **As I live, saith the Lord GOD,
> I have no pleasure in the death of the wicked;**
> but that **the wicked turn from his way and
> live**: **turn ye, turn ye from your evil ways**; for
> **why will ye die**…?"

No matter your previous religion, you must now be **willing
to forsake your sins, turn to God** and **ask for His forgiveness
in order to receive His Salvation. Sin and its decaying effects
remain on those who refuse to repent** and at the end of their
lives, God will hold them accountable for their sins. The reason
is because, **God does not acquit a guilty person** who refuses
to repent of his or her sins **after hearing the Good News of
the Gospel.** He told us this when He introduced Himself to
Moses in **Exodus 34:7:**

> "*(God)* **Keeping mercy for thousands, forgiving iniquity
> and transgression and sin** *(of those who repent);* **and
> that** **will by no means clear the guilty** *(those who do
> not repent)* **visiting the iniquity of the fathers upon
> the children, and upon the children's children,** unto
> the third and to the fourth generation."

Those who reject His Salvation in Christ will face His wrath
when they die; they shall be damned. Unfortunately, **a lot of
people who choose for whatever reason not to believe in
Christ are in this category that God will not acquit of their sins.**

How to Make the Lord Jesus Your Savior

**If you want to make the Lord Jesus your Savior, you can
do it right now.** Again, you **must believe** the Good News of
the Word of God in **John 3:16-18:**

> "**For God so loved the world, that he gave his only
> begotten Son, that whosoever believeth in him
> should not perish, but have everlasting life.**
>
> 17 For God sent not his Son into the world to
> condemn the world; **but that the world through**

him might be saved. *18* <u>He that believeth on him is not condemned</u>: but he that believeth not is condemned already, because he hath not believed in the name of the only begotten Son of God."

When you **believe this in your heart, confess with your mouth that the Lord Jesus died for your sins, was buried and God raised Him from the dead, you shall be saved** as stated in **Romans 10:9-10:**

"That if thou shalt **confess with thy mouth the Lord Jesus,** and shalt **believe in thine heart that God hath raised him from the dead, thou shalt be saved.** *10* For with the heart man believeth unto righteousness; and with the mouth confession is made unto salvation."

Repent of your sins, ask Him for forgiveness of all your sins and invite Him to come into your heart to be your Lord; **ask Him to give you the Holy Spirit**.

Pray this Prayer below **aloud** if you **believe** what is written in the Scriptures above:

The Prayer of Salvation

"Father God, in the name of the Lord Jesus, I come to You because **I believe that Jesus Christ is Your Son. I believe that He came into the world in the flesh and that He was crucified on the Cross for my sins; <u>He died on the Cross for my sins, was buried and on the third day, You raised Him from the dead</u>**. Today, I confess it with my mouth because I believe it in my heart. **Lord Jesus, I repent of all my sins and I ask You to forgive me all my sins. Please, come into my heart and be my Lord** for I surrender to Your Lordship this day and forever. I choose Your eternal life and I declare that I belong to You from now on.

I also ask You to <u>give me Your Holy Spirit</u> to teach me the Bible, lead, protect and keep me safe from now on.

I choose to do only those things that please You from now on. Father, I believe that You heard me and that I am now your child. Thank You for giving me Your Son and Your Holy Spirit. Father, in the name of the Lord Jesus, into Your hands I now commit my life; spirit, soul and body for safe keeping; Amen."

Congratulations on making the Lord Jesus the Lord of your life. Now, study the Bible and **trust God to keep you; even if it means being put to physical death by the forces of the antichrist.** Again, know that you will go to Heaven and not hell because **you chose to belong to the Lord Jesus and not the antichrist**. He will give you a new body.

What You Receive When You Come to Christ

Below are some of the blessings you will receive from God when you make the Lord Jesus your Lord and Savior:

1. **He Washes Away Your Sins**

   When you come to Christ, repent of your sins and ask Him to forgive your sins, He washes away *(forgives)* your sins with His blood. God fulfills His promise to you in **Isaiah 1:18** to cleanse you from all your sins; no matter how horrible they are:

   > "Come now, and let us reason together, saith the LORD: **though your sins be as scarlet, they shall be as white as snow; <u>though they be red like crimson</u>, they shall be as wool**."

   Having your sins washed away by the Blood of the Lord Jesus means that you are now **a child of God** and that you are now **Heaven bound instead of hell**. Meaning that, all those who hold on to their sins by rejecting Jesus, are hell bound.

2. **He Reconciles You to God**

   When you come to the Lord Jesus Christ, He reconciles you with the Almighty God; His Father—**2 Corinthians 5:19-20:**

   > "To wit *(know)*, that <u>**God was in Christ, reconciling the world unto himself**</u>, not imputing their **trespasses unto them**; and hath committed unto

us the word of reconciliation. 20 Now then we are ambassadors for Christ, as though God did beseech you by us: **we pray you in Christ's stead, be ye reconciled to God."**

3. You Become Born Again

By receiving the Lord Jesus as your personal Lord and Savior, you became <u>Born Again</u> which is the Lord's requirement for seeing the Kingdom of God as we see in **John 3:3** *(it means that you are reborn by the Spirit of God in Christ)*:

> "Jesus answered and said unto him, Verily, verily, I say unto thee, **except a man be <u>Born Again,</u> he cannot see the kingdom of God."**

You become an heir of God; a joint-heir with Christ. It means you become entitled to all that God owns; all things!

4. He Gives You the Gift of Eternal Life

It is **Good News** that you believe in the Lord Jesus Christ and that you have placed your **faith in Him.** Therefore, you will not perish but receive the Gift of Eternal Life; **God's life will begin to work in you — John 3:16:**

> "For God so loved the world, that he gave his only begotten Son, that **whosoever believeth in him should not perish, but <u>have everlasting life</u>** *(Eternal Life)."*

5. He Gives You the Gift of the Holy Sprit

All those who come to the Lord Jesus are **sealed by the Holy Spirit** so, when **you believe and confess Him as your Lord,** He will <u>seal you with the Holy Spirit</u> — **Ephesians 1:13-14:**

> "In whom ye also trusted, after that ye heard the word of truth, the gospel of your salvation: **in whom also after that ye believed, <u>ye were sealed</u> with that holy Spirit of promise,** 14 Which is the <u>**earnest of our inheritance**</u> *(down payment)* until the redemption of the purchased possession, unto the praise of his glory."

6. He Makes You One with Him and with God the Father

The Lord Jesus asked God the Father to make us one with them as we see in **John 17:21-23:**

> "That they all *(believers)* may be one; as thou, Father, art in me, and I in thee, that **they also may be one in us**: that the world may believe that thou hast sent me… 23 **I in them, and You in Me; that they may be made perfect in one, and that the world may know that You have sent Me, and have loved them as You have loved Me.**"

7. He Makes You a King and a Priest of God

The Lord Jesus does not only make you a child of God, He also makes you a King and a Priest unto God. This qualifies you as a Priest to offer Sacrifices of Praise to God and as a King to rule on earth over all Principalities, Powers, Rulers of the darkness of this world and their spiritual wickedness; meaning the devil and all his evil forces — **Revelation 5:10:**

> "And hast made us unto our God **kings and priests**: and we shall reign on the earth."

8. He Gives You His Power and Authority to Rule in His Name

The Lord gives you the Power and Authority to use His Name — **Luke 10:19:**

> "Behold, **I give unto you power to tread on serpents and scorpions** *(demons)*, **and over all the power of the enemy** *(devil)*: **and nothing shall by any means hurt you.**"

And in **Mark 16:17-18:**

> "And these signs shall follow them that believe; **In my Name shall they cast out devils**; they shall speak with new tongues; 18 **They shall take up serpents; and if they drink any deadly thing, it shall not hurt them; they shall lay hands on the sick, and they shall recover.**"

Chapter 6
What to Do if You Were Left Behind after Rapture

All Things are Possible with God

I stated before that to be left behind means that **you were not 'caught-up' by the Lord Jesus when He came to take away faithful Christians and innocent children from the earth**; it means you missed Rapture. This does not mean that God has given up on you because with our God, all things are possible. The Lord Jesus told us this in **Mark 10:27:**

> "And Jesus looking upon them saith, <u>with men it is impossible</u>, **but not with God**: <u>for with God all things are possible</u>."

This means that the Lord can still save all those who place their trust in Him and **do not take the Mark of the Beast because of the fear of physical death.** Therefore, let this scripture above **encourage you** when the devil is telling you that **you have no hope because you missed Rapture.** Always remember that, "with God all things are possible" and that <u>He will become a way for you</u> when there is no way as long as you trust Him.

Again, the Lord will always be with **all those who place their trust in Him even during the Great Tribulation but anyone who takes the Mark of the Beast will be damned to hell forever; nothing can be done for them**. The Lord loves you dearly and wants you to choose Him so that you can be in Heaven. Know that you are not alone and that even the multitudes in Heaven are praying for you and cheering you on; God loves you.

What to Do to Protect Yourself and Others

Make sure that you are reconciled with God by the blood of the Lord Jesus Christ. Always remember that the **antichrist** or the **Beast** is an **agent of the devil.** As a result:

1. **Do not believe anything** he or the **false prophet** say; they are **liars** and **deceivers**
2. Now is the time for you to **learn how to call on the name of the Lord** daily
3. Do not take the **Mark of the Beast** or **the number of his name** which is **666**

4. **Be steadfast** and do not loose heart
5. All is not lost when you have the Lord Jesus; **He is all you need**
6. **Do not give up** or compromise **your new or renewed faith** in Christ
7. Remember that you were **left behind** because **you did not believe or take the Lord's promises seriously** as you ought to; **do not make the same mistake again**
8. **Repent and ask God for forgiveness for not accepting, not believing or for compromising your belief** in the Lord Jesus before Rapture
9. **Forgive yourself** for this
10. **Do not kill yourself** because doing so will put you in hell; Jesus does not let anyone into heaven who killed themselves
11. **Ask Him to be your Lord and Savior** (see **John 3:16** and **Romans 10:9-10** in the Bible)
12. **Get to know God the Father, the Lord Jesus and the Lord Holy Spirit** by studying the Word (the Bible)
13. **Pray and worship God** in the name of the Lord Jesus
14. **Call on the Lord Jesus when you are in trouble**, danger or afraid; He will answer you once you belong to Him
15. **Be faithful unto death**; do not fear physical death because **spiritual death in hell is worse**
16. **Your loved ones who died in Christ or were raptured are waiting for you**
17. Make your goal Heaven knowing there is great love and joy for you there

What You Must Not Do at this Time
1. **Do not be Angry with God**

Do not get angry with God for being left behind; **He sent you His Son and His children on earth to tell you about what will happen to those who did not take their Christian walk seriously, rejected the Message of Salvation or did not believe the Bible was the Word of God.** Be honest with yourself that it is not God's fault but your own.

Tell yourself that it is time to repent of all your sins and ask God to forgive you of all your sins. Ask the Lord Jesus to be your Lord and to give you His Holy Spirit to keep you through the terrible things that are happening in your new world.

2. Do Not Dwell on Blaming Yourself

Do not dwell in blaming yourself for missing Rapture but **dwell in the Hope that you can still choose to have faith in Christ. Be fully persuaded that God is with you because you have placed your trust in Him and that <u>He will never leave you nor forsake you</u>.** Remind yourself that **He is faithful to keep you even if you are killed physically** because physical death only means that you will go to spend eternity with God in Heaven.

3. It is Time to Remember the Cross

It is the time for you to remember the Cross of the Lord Jesus Christ. As you are aware, God loves us so much that He sent His only begotten Son Jesus *(whom He also loves so much)* to die on the Cross for our sins. **No one saw the love of God among all those who were looking as the Lord Jesus was crucified and hanging on the Cross in agony.**

No one understood what both God the Father and the Lord Jesus were doing for humanity in what was going on. It is afterwards that the Lord opened our understanding in **Isaiah 53:2-11** to **reveal God's accomplishment for us in Christ on the Cross**:

> "...**He** *(Jesus)* **hath no form nor comeliness; and when we shall see him, there is no beauty that we should desire him** *(He was not handsome).* 3 **He is despised and rejected of men; a man of sorrows, and acquainted with grief**: and <u>we hid as it were our faces from him</u>; he was despised, and <u>we esteemed him not</u> *(we did not honor or hold Him in High regards).*
>
> 4 **Surely he hath borne our griefs, and carried our sorrows**: yet we did esteem him stricken, **smitten of God, and afflicted.** 5 **But he was <u>wounded for our transgressions, he was bruised for our iniquities</u>: <u>the chastisement of our peace was upon him</u>** *(He received the punishment to get us peace);* **and <u>with his stripes we are healed</u>** *(Each stripe He received was payment for our healing).*
>
> 6 All we like sheep have gone astray; we have turned everyone to his own way; and the LORD

hath laid on him the iniquity of us all. 7 **He was oppressed, and he was afflicted, yet he opened not his mouth: he is brought as a lamb to the slaughter, and as a sheep before her shearers is dumb, so he openeth not his mouth.**

8 He was taken from prison and from judgment: and who shall declare his generation? **for he was cut off out of the land of the living** *(He died for our sins)*: **for the transgression of my people was he stricken.** 9 And he made his grave with the wicked, and with the rich in his death; **because he had done no violence, neither was any deceit in his mouth** *(a sinless Lamb worthy to be sacrificed for human sins).*

10 **Yet it pleased the LORD to bruise him** *(God was pleased that His Lamb was worthy to be sacrificed);* **he hath put him to grief: when thou shalt make his soul an offering for sin, he shall see his seed** *(Christians),* **he shall prolong his days** *(Christians shall preach the Good News of His purchased salvation for the world),* **and the pleasure of the LORD shall prosper in his hand.**

11 **He shall see of the travail of his soul, and shall be satisfied** *(He shall be pleased when He sees His sufferings and death resulting in the salvation of all who believe and place their trust in Him):* **by his knowledge shall my righteous servant justify many; for he shall bear their iniquities** *(He saves many from their sins and iniquities by our preaching the Gospel to them)."*

This is why you must still trust Him because His ways are not our ways. You do not know how He will use your persecution and death in the age to come. Know that right now, you and all the faithful Christians in your new world ruled by the wicked, are now God's vessels to tell all those who have not yet received the Lord that it is not too late for anyone to turn to Christ.

Unfortunately for those unwilling to turn to Christ but choose to persecute Christians, they will find out at the end that their actions have doomed their souls forever. They do not yet know that **the Christians that they are killing right now will all be testimonies against them that they chose evil over good when they are judged by Christ.** Therefore, remember the Lord's Word in **Matthew 10:21-26.** He knew that these things will happen:

> "And **the brother shall deliver up the brother to death, and the father the child:** and **the children shall rise up against their parents, and cause them to be put to death.** 22 And **ye shall be hated of all men for my name's sake:** but **he that endureth to the end shall be saved.**
>
> 23 But when they persecute you in this city, flee ye into another: for verily I say unto you, Ye shall not have gone over the cities of Israel, till the Son of man be come. 24 **The disciple is not above his master, nor the servant above his lord.**
>
> 25 **It is enough for the disciple that he be as his master, and the servant as his lord. If they have called the master of the house Beelzebub, how much more shall they call them of his household?** 26 **Fear them not therefore**: for there is nothing covered, that shall not be revealed; and hid, that shall not be known."

4. **Do not Dwell in Your Past**
   Everyone's past is full of areas where they failed so do not dwell in your past. Instead, walk with the "**Mind of Christ**" *(thinking upon God's Word always)* and as the Apostle Paul advised us in **Philippians 4:8:**

> "Finally, brethren, whatsoever **things are true,** whatsoever **things are honest,** whatsoever **things are just,** whatsoever **things are pure,** whatsoever **things are lovely,** whatsoever **things are of good report**; if there be **any virtue,** and if there be **any praise, think on these things.**"

Learn to fill your mind with the things listed in the above scripture. Do not let your mind stray to negative thoughts. It will help you to meditate on **Philippians 3:7-14:**

"But <u>what things were gain to me, those I counted loss for Christ.</u> *8* **Yea doubtless, and I count all things but loss for the excellency of the knowledge of Christ Jesus my Lord**: for whom I have suffered the loss of all things, and do count them but dung, that I may win Christ,

9 And be found in him, not having mine own righteousness, which is of the law, but that which is through the faith of Christ, the righteousness which is of God by faith: *10* **That I may know him, and the power of his resurrection, and the fellowship of his sufferings, being made conformable unto his death;** *11* If by any means I might attain unto the resurrection of the dead

12 Not as though I had already attained, either were already perfect: but I follow after, if that I may apprehend that for which also I am apprehended of Christ Jesus. *13* Brethren, I count not myself to have apprehended: **but <u>this one thing I do, forgetting those things which are behind, and reaching forth unto those things which are before</u>,** *14* **<u>I press toward the mark for the prize of the high calling of God in Christ Jesus</u>** *(there is a Prize for finishing well in Christ)*."

The **Apostle Paul's desire was to be killed the same way that Christ was killed.** He wanted to experience the same type of suffering Christ did so that he can experience His resurrection power. **Now that you are in the Great Tribulation period, you may go through what Paul desired to go through which is be killed for Christ! <u>Salvation is Free but there is always a price for following the Lord Jesus and sometimes, that price is your Life.</u>** Remember what the Lord said in **Luke 9:62:**

"And Jesus said unto him, **No man, having put his hand to the plough, and looking back, is fit for the kingdom of God.**"

The only time the Lord told us to check out the past is in **Luke 17:32** when He said "**Remember Lot's wife.**" She looked back and became a pillar of salt! **Again, do not dwell on your past but press on to receive the prize God has for you in Christ.**

Obey the Message of Salvation

If you have never made the Lord Jesus your Savior, **you can do it right now. To receive the Lord Jesus as your Savior, pray the Prayer of Salvation below;** you must first **believe** the **Good News** of the **Gospel** in **John 3:16-17:**

> **"For God so loved the world,** that <u>he gave his only begotten Son,</u> that <u>whosoever believeth in him should not perish, but have everlasting life.</u> 17 For God sent not his Son into the world to condemn the world; but that the world through him might be saved."**

You must also believe that **the Lord Jesus is the <u>only way that you can get to God in Heaven</u>** as stated in **Acts 4:12:**

> **"Neither is there salvation in any other: for there is <u>none other name</u> *(than the name of Jesus)* <u>under heaven given among men, whereby we must be saved."</u>**

We are told in **Romans 10:9-10** that when we believe in our hearts and confess the Lordship of Christ with our mouths, we shall be saved:

> "That if thou shalt **confess with thy mouth the Lord Jesus, and shalt believe in thine heart that God hath raised him from the dead,** thou **shalt be saved.** 10 For **with the heart man believeth unto righteousness; and with the mouth confession is made unto salvation."**

The Prayer of Salvation

"Father, in the name of the Lord Jesus, I come to you and **I believe that Jesus Christ is Your Son. I believe that He came into the world in the flesh and that He was crucified on the Cross for my sins. He died on the Cross for my sins and was buried but on the third day, You raised Him from the dead.**

Today, I confess it with my mouth and I believe it in my heart. Lord Jesus, **I repent of all my sins, I ask You to forgive me all my sins and wash me of my sins with Your blood. Please, come into my heart and be my Lord** for I surrender to Your Lordship this day and forever. Give me Your eternal life for I declare that I belong to You from now on.

Also, I ask You to **give me Your Holy Spirit** to keep me in Your will, teach me the Bible, lead and protect me. I choose to do only those things that please You from now on. Father, I believe that You heard me and that I am now your child. Thank You for giving me Your Son and Your Holy Spirit. I receive them in the name of the Lord Jesus; Amen."

It is a **big deal** to make the Lord Jesus your Lord and Savior. In **John 3:18-21**, we are told that some people who rejected the **love of God** that He **sent to Humanity in His Son Jesus Christ will be condemned to hell:**

> "He that believeth on him is not condemned: **but he that believeth not is condemned already, because he hath not believed in the name of the only begotten Son of God.** *19* And **this is the condemnation, that light is come into the world, and men loved darkness rather than light, because their deeds were evil.**
>
> *20* **For every one that doeth evil hateth the light, neither cometh to the light, lest his deeds should be reproved.** *21* But he that doeth truth cometh to the light, that his deeds may be made manifest, that they are wrought in God."

Again, all who choose the antichrist will burn in **hell** and the **Lake of Fire.** By now, you know **that the Bible tells the truth about these things** so, keep your **faith** and **light** burning bright in the dark-world that you now find yourself.

Chapter 7
What Those Left Behind Will Face in the 'New World'

Those Left Behind

If you are one of those left behind, know that there will be great hardships happening on earth because of the **Seals of Judgment and of God pouring out His wrath on the wicked, the hypocrites and those who rejected His Son.** Therefore, you will experience some of these events but, you still have to hold onto God because again, **it is not too late for you yet; you can still receive the Lord Jesus and be saved.**

God Seals His Children before Pouring Out His Wrath

I want you to know that **God places His Seal or His Mark of protection on the foreheads of His children** (*those who believe in Christ and made Him their Lord*) before pouring out His wrath of judgment upon those on earth. As a result, **besides the 144 thousand souls that will be sealed from the tribes of Israel, He will also place His Seal upon you** as recorded in **Revelation 7:2-9:**

> "And I saw another angel ascending from the east, **having the seal of the living God**: and he cried with a loud voice to the four angels, to whom it was given to hurt the earth and the sea, 3 Saying, **Hurt not the earth, neither the sea, nor the trees, till we have sealed the servants of our God in their foreheads** (*Tribulation Saints*)...
>
> 9 After this **I beheld, and, lo, a great multitude, which no man could number, of all nations, and kindreds, and people, and tongues**, stood before the throne, and before the Lamb, clothed with white robes, and palms in their hands."

After you are sealed, you become one of the above multitudes that came out of the **Great Tribulation.** Be assured that if you belong to the Lord Jesus at this time, God is on your side and He will be with you. Therefore, do not be despaired because the Lord **can still keep you at this time and guide you towards Heaven.** Keep reminding yourself that that even those who endure physical death for the sake of the Lord Jesus, shall be saved.

The Beginning of God's Wrath

The Lord Jesus as the Lamb of God will judge the earth because God the Father has committed all judgment into His Hand — **John 5:22-23**:

> "For the Father judgeth no man, but hath committed all judgment unto the Son: 23 That all men should honour the Son, even as they honour the Father. He that honoureth not the Son honoureth not the Father which hath sent him."

As a result, you are now experiencing what the Bible says will happen; events such as **stars falling** from the **sky to the earth** and **mountains moved out of their places.** It will be a time of great calamities and all those who dwell on earth will experience **God's judgments and wrath.** For example, we see what happens when one of the seals is opened in **Revelation 6:12-17**:

> "**And I beheld when he had opened the sixth seal,** and, lo, there was a great earthquake; and the sun became black as sackcloth of hair, **and the moon became as blood;** And **the <u>stars of heaven fell unto the earth</u>,** even as a fig tree casteth her untimely figs, when she is shaken of a mighty wind. 14 And **the heaven departed as a scroll when it is rolled together;** and <u>**every mountain and island**</u> were <u>**moved out of their places**</u>.
>
> 15 And the **kings of the earth,** and the **great men,** and the **rich men,** and the **chief captains,** and the **mighty men,** and **every bondman,** and **every free man,** hid themselves in the dens and in the rocks of the mountains; 16 And **said to the mountains and rocks, fall on us,** and <u>**hide us from the face of him that sitteth on the throne**</u>, and from the wrath of the Lamb *(Jesus Christ):* 17 For **the great day of his wrath is come;** and who shall be able to stand?"

More wrath will be poured out upon all those who rejected the gift of God's Son Jesus Christ and the Salvation He brought to humanity. For instance, there will be no wind on earth — **Revelation 7:1-2:**

> "And after these things **I saw four angels standing on the four corners of the earth, holding the four winds of the earth, <u>that the wind should not blow on the earth</u>, nor on the sea, nor on any tree.** 2 And I saw another angel ascending from the east, having the seal of the living God: and he cried with a loud voice to **the four angels, <u>to whom it was given to hurt the earth and the sea</u>...**"

Unbearable Hardship

Apart from the calamities coming upon the earth from the sky, you may already begin to feel great hardship upon the earth. **Know that these hardships will not get any better because God is giving those who rejected Him a taste of what life on earth is like without Him.** He is allowing man to see what the devil has to offer those who choose him instead of God.

Therefore, as you are seeing in your new world, **wicked men and women are now in charge** and as a result, those left behind on earth are living an unbearable life under them. People will suffer or go through:

1. **Great fear**
2. Cold, lack of food, water, danger in society at large
3. **Persecution** of Christians
4. **Living in hiding** at different locations
5. The rise of the **antichrist**; the future world leader
6. People taking the **Mark in order to eat** will be damned forever
7. **Lack of peace** due to wars and devastations
8. **Plagues** and famines and diseases, etc.

What the Lord said about the Great Tribulation Period

The Lord Jesus forewarned us about **the Days of Tribulation** by telling us that **the hardship will be worse than anything ever felt on earth** —Matthew 24:21-22:

> "For then **shall be great tribulation, such as was not since the beginning of the world to this time, no, nor ever shall be.** 22 And <u>except those days should be shortened, there should no flesh be saved</u>: but for the elect's sake those days shall be shortened."

Summary of God's Judgments with the 7 Seals

As **the Lord Jesus begins to judge all those on earth,** each of the Seven (7) Seals that He opens will unleash a different calamity. These seals are affixed *(stamped)* on the Scroll that contains God's judgement. Below is the summary of the judgments as recorded in **Revelation 6:1-17.** The first four seals release the '4 Horsemen of the Apocalypse' who bring great destruction on earth.

Seal #1: Revelation 6:1-2:

"…I saw when **the Lamb opened one of the seals,** and I heard, as it were the noise of thunder, one of the four beasts saying, Come and see. 2 **And I saw, and behold a white horse: and he that sat on him had a bow; and a crown was given unto him: and he went forth conquering, and to conquer.**"

The rider of the white horse is the antichrist or the future world leader who will be the devil's most wicked vessel that deals ruthlessly with all those under him. He will dominate *(conquer)* the whole world for 7 years.

Seal #2: Revelation 6:3-4:

"And when **he had opened the second seal,** I heard the second beast say, Come and see. 4 And there **went out another horse that was red: and <u>power was given to him that sat thereon to take peace from the earth,</u> and that <u>they should kill one another:</u> and <u>there was given unto him a great sword</u>** *(watch out for the radical Muslims seeking to behead people).*"

People will begin to kill one another in wars, religious persecutions and those refusing to worship the antichrist by rejecting his Mark, will provoke him to **unleash all kinds of wickedness against them** as he reigns.

Seal #3: Revelation 6:5-6:

"And when **he had opened the third seal,** I heard the third beast say, Come and see. And I beheld, and lo **a black horse; and he that sat on him had a pair of balances in his hand.** 6 And I heard a voice in the midst of the four beasts say, **A measure of wheat for a penny, and three measures of barley for a penny;** and see thou hurt not the oil and the wine."

This <u>rider of the black horse</u> **brings famine on earth**. Millions of people will starve to death all over the world.

Seal #4: Revelation 6:7-8:

"And when **he had opened the fourth seal**, I heard the voice of the fourth beast say, Come and see. *8* And I looked, and behold **a pale horse: and his name that sat on him was Death, and hell followed with him.** And **power was given unto them over the fourth part of the earth, to kill with sword, and with hunger, and with death, and with the beasts of the earth."**

This <u>rider of the pale horse</u> **brings death and hell on earth** with it. More people will die from a combination of wars, famines and other forms of killing. Animals will turn against people and kill them.

Seal #5: Revelation 6:9-11:

"And when **he had opened the fifth seal, I saw under the altar the souls of them that were <u>slain for the word of God,</u> and for the testimony which they held** (*Those who did not deny their Faith in Christ even when faced with death*): *10* And they cried with a loud voice, saying, How long, O Lord, holy and true, dost thou not judge and a venge our blood on them that dwell on the earth?

11 And white robes were given unto every one of them; and it was said unto them, that **they should rest yet for a little season, until their fellowservants also and their brethren, that should be killed as they were, should be fulfilled** (*meaning those who will be killed during the tribulation that you are now in*)."

The opening of the **5ᵗʰ Seal <u>reveals how those who died for the Word of God</u>** (*martyred for their faith in Christ*) **did not perish.** Instead, they are waiting for their fellow Brethren that will also be **martyred** by the antichrist and his forces. <u>God intends to **judge the devil, his forces and all who sided with him** to persecute and kill His children</u> on earth. He will make them pay **from the blood of righteous Abel killed by Cain** to the <u>blood of the last believer</u> that will be martyred.

Therefore, know and be **assured that God has not forsaken even those who will be killed in the days that you are now** in. **Your duty now is to hold on to your faith in Christ even if it means your physical death and you will receive your reward in Christ.** It is no time to lose hope.

Seal #6: Revelation 6:12-17:

"And I beheld when **he had opened the sixth seal, and, lo, there was a great earthquake; and the sun became black as sackcloth of hair, and the moon became as blood;** 13 And **the stars of heaven fell unto the earth,** even as a fig tree casteth her untimely figs, when she is shaken of a mighty wind.

14 And **the heaven departed as a scroll when it is rolled together; and every mountain and island were moved out of their places.** 15 And **the kings of the earth, and the great men, and the rich men, and the chief captains, and the mighty men, and every bondman, and every free man,** hid themselves in the dens and in the rocks of the mountains; 16 **And said to the mountains and rocks, <u>fall on us</u>, and <u>hide us</u> from the face of him that <u>sitteth on the throne</u>, and from the wrath of the Lamb:** 17 **For the <u>great day of his wrath is come</u>;** and who shall be able to stand?"

Seal #7: Revelation 8:1-6:

"**And when he had opened the seventh seal, there was silence in heaven about the space of half an hour.** 2 And I saw the seven angels which stood before God; and to them were given seven trumpets... 6 And the seven angels which had the seven trumpets prepared themselves to sound."

Summary of God's Judgments with the Seven (7) Trumpets

There will be an **additional 7 trumpets of Judgments** and as each trumpet sounds, more of the wrath of God will be poured out on earth as we see in **Revelation 8:7-13:**

Trumpet #1

"7 The first angel sounded, and **there followed hail and fire mingled with blood, and they were cast upon the earth:** and the third part of trees was burnt up, and all green grass was burnt up."

This hailstorm will destroy a third of the trees and grass on earth so that there will be scarcity of green-vegetation. The implication of this is that there will be little or no food that can grow in a third of the earth. Therefore, more people will begin to starve for lack of food.

Trumpet #2

"8 And the second angel sounded, and as it were **a great mountain burning with fire was cast into the sea: and the third part of the sea became blood;** 9 And the third part of the creatures which were in the sea, and had life, died; and the third part of the ships were destroyed."

There will be destruction and death on earth when the water in the sea turns to blood because an object like a meteorite or asteroid is cast into the sea and kills a third of all marine life *(fish)*. There will be scarcity of seafood.

Trumpet #3

"10 And the third angel sounded, and **there fell a great star from heaven, burning as it were a lamp, and it fell upon the third part of the rivers, and upon the fountains of waters;** 11 And the name of the star is **called Wormwood**: and the third part of the waters became wormwood; **and many men died of the waters, because they were made bitter."**

There will be scarcity of fresh water so that at this time, not only are people dying from famine, they will begin to die from thirst as well.

Trumpet #4

"12 And the fourth angel sounded, and **the third part of the sun was smitten, and the third part of the moon, and the third part of the stars; so as the third part of them was darkened, and the day shone not for a third part of it, and the night likewise.** 13 And I beheld, and heard an angel flying through the midst of heaven, saying with a loud voice, **Woe, woe, woe, to the inhabiters of the earth by reason of the other voices of the trumpet of the three angels, which are yet to sound!"**

The earth will become cold, gloomy and lawlessness will abound as life will become everyman for himself in all the nations. To make matters worse, when the 'Four Angels' that are currently **chained in the river Euphrates are loosed,** they will kill millions of people — **Revelation 9:14-15:**

> "Saying to the sixth angel which had the trumpet, Loose the four angels *(Death Angels)* which are bound in the great river Euphrates. 15 And the four angels were loosed, which **were prepared for an hour, and a day, and a month, and a year, for to slay the third part of men** *(the world population)*."

God's wrath is not over yet; there are more judgments to come.

Additional Judgments by Seven (7) Vials

The **last judgments are poured out of 7 Vials.** Life on earth will become even more unbearable as people are scorched by heat from the sun, have to drink blood for water while they endure painful sores as **Revelation 16:1-11** unfolds:

> "And I heard a great voice out of the temple saying to the seven angels, Go your ways, and pour out the vials of the wrath of God upon the earth. 2 And the first went, and poured out his vial upon the earth; and **there fell a noisome and grievous sore upon the men which had the mark of the beast, and upon them which worshipped his image.**
>
> 3 And **the second angel poured out his vial upon the sea;** and **it became as the blood of a dead man:** and every living soul died in the sea. 4 And **the third angel poured out his vial upon the rivers and fountains of waters;** and **they became blood.**
>
> 5 And I heard the angel of the waters say, Thou art righteous, O Lord, which art, and wast, and shalt be, because thou hast judged thus. 6 **For they have shed the blood of saints and prophets, and thou hast given them blood to drink;** for **they are worthy.** 7 And I heard another out of the altar say, Even so, Lord God Almighty, true and righteous are thy judgments.
>
> 8 And **the fourth angel poured out his vial upon the sun;** and **power was given unto him to scorch men**

with fire. 9 And **men were scorched with great heat, and blasphemed the name of God, which hath power over these plagues**: and they repented not to give him glory.

10 And **the fifth angel poured out his vial upon the seat of the beast** *(the antichrist);* and **his kingdom was full of darkness**; and **they** *(all who took his Mark)* **gnawed their tongues for pain,** 11 And blasphemed the God of heaven because of **their pains and their sores,** and repented not of their deeds."

People will be Unable to Die

As **calamities and plagues** are being poured upon the wicked on the earth and **all those who took the Mark of the Beast will seek death in those days and cannot find it**. This is because **death will be powerless to kill them**; they will suffer but not die — **Revelation 9:6:**

"And **in those days shall men seek death, and shall not find it**; and shall desire to die, and **death shall flee from them.**"

Do not Join the Wicked Ones

At this time, famines, wars, calamities from the sky and evil angels will leave dead bodies everywhere in the world. People will be running in their attempts to escape these things but they cannot hide. Houses and buildings everywhere will be destroyed and there will be lawlessness and wickedness everywhere. **As for you, do not join the wicked because if you do, you will be judged** along with them as recorded in **Revelation 21:8:**

"But the **fearful, and unbelieving, and the abominable, and murderers, and whoremongers, and sorcerers, and idolaters, and all liars, shall have their part in the lake which burneth with fire and brimstone: which is the second death.**"

The Bible tells us about **God's Great Judgment** *(on individuals)* that is **waiting for all the wicked.** Everyone will stand before Christ and be judged for their actions after Christ's Millennial Reign according to **Revelation 20:11-15:**

"And **I saw a great white throne, and him that sat on it, from whose face the earth and the heaven fled away;** and there was found no place for them. *12* **And I saw the dead, small and great, stand before God;** and the books were opened: and another book was opened, which is the book of life:

and the dead were judged out of those things which were written in the books, according to their works. *13* And **the sea gave up the dead which were in it;** and **death and hell delivered up the dead which were in them: and they were judged every man according to their works.**

14 And death and hell were cast into the lake of fire. **This is the second death** *(being eternally separated from God and His goodness and be burned forever)*. *15* **And whosoever was not found written in the book of life was cast into the lake of fire."**

This is why the Lord said in **Revelation 22:11-12:**

"**He that is unjust, let him be unjust still: and he which is filthy, let him be filthy still: and he that is righteous, let him be righteous still: and he that is holy, let him be holy still.** *12* **And, behold, I come quickly; and my reward is with me, to give every man according as his work shall be."**

Do you now see why everyone should commit their lives to Jesus Christ? He will reward every person for his or her deeds on earth; there shall be no escape from His judgment.

Those Who Accept the Lord at this Time

Finally, I say again, that **God is able to keep you because He made provisions for you to come to Him** before His Second Coming in 7 years after Rapture. He is returning to judge the wicked, reign and rule on earth for a thousand years! It is not too late for those who accept Christ at this time. **Make Him your Lord and learn to call on and run to Him when you are in trouble.**

Chapter 8
Rise of the Antichrist and One World Government

Why will God allow the Antichrist to Rule the World?

If you notice, the average man or woman blames God when things go wrong in their lives; they hold God responsible for their misfortune. The reason for this is because they do not have a revelation of the devil or satan and his destructive ways in human life. Therefore, they ask: **Why does God allow so much evil in the world?** The answer is very simple as you already saw.

Adam's Misuse of Free Will

In the previous chapter, we saw that when God created **Adam** *(man)*, **He gave man a free will** and **He instructed him to stay away from the Tree of the Knowledge of Good and Evil because its fruit will kill him.** God told Adam this because He did not want Adam to ever taste or experience evil which results in death and eternal separation from God.

We saw that when the devil came on the scene as <u>a serpent</u>, he told the Woman *(Eve; Adam's wife)* that <u>God had lied to her and her husband;</u> because God did not want them to become like gods. **He also told her that the fruit of the Tree will make them Wise so that they can know** *(experience)* **good and evil. The devil wanted Adam and Eve to** <u>taste</u> or <u>experience evil</u> contrary to God's will.

God Honored Man's Choice of the Devil as His Lord

Eve believed the devil's lies rather than God's Word to them *(the only Truth there is)* **and she began to lust after the fruit. She took the fruit and ate it which resulted in sin and corruption.** To make matters worse, when **Adam whom God had made the Lord of the Earth** *(to exercise Dominion on earth)* came to his wife Eve, she offered him the **Fruit.**

Knowing full well what God told him about the result of eating the fruit *(death),* **Adam of his own free will** <u>accepted the fruit</u> from his wife and <u>he ate it</u>. God honors man's free will so that when he chose to experience evil, God honored his choice. In choosing evil, Adam *(the Lord of the Earth)* tasted evil or experienced evil for himself and for **everyone that came out of his loins; meaning all humanity! By choosing a Union with the devil instead of God, Adam** yielded his 'authority' as Lord of the Earth to the devil.

Romans 6:16 explains to us **what happened when Adam yielded his Lordship and authority to the devil;** it made him a servant to the devil:

> "**Know ye not, that to whom ye yield yourselves servants to obey,** his servants ye are to whom ye obey**; whether of sin unto death,** or of **obedience** *(obedience to God's Word)* **unto righteousness?**"

As soon as Adam lost his Lordship over the earth to the devil, **the devil promptly unleashed evil and wickedness against humanity who suddenly became his subjects since the 'Adamic Authority'** now belongs to him. As servants of the devil *(compliments of Adam)*, humanity has been experiencing the evil nature of the devil since Adam.

This is why the gross evil, wickedness, wars, diseases, pre-mature deaths and destruction that you see in the world today are the direct result of the devil exacting his evil rule over humanity. Therefore, in answering the question of why there is evil in the world, you can now see that it was **Man's** *(Adam)* **desire** and **choice** to **taste** or **experience evil** even after **God told him that evil will kill him.** This is why the evil you now see in the world is not from God but from man's choice.

Man Has Not Changed Since Adam

What is shocking is that man has not changed since Adam because people continue to ignore God's instructions (*His Word in the Bible***) and walk in the devil's evil ways.** Again, do not blame God for the evil in the world; it was man's choice and many people still delight themselves in evil. For example, as I stated before the reason you were not '**caught**

up' at Rapture by **Christ** was because of **how you responded to the Word of God preached** to you.

Many people were **under delusion** *(from family, friends, secular humanism, etc.)* and as a result, **did not receive the Word of God** that **Christ was their way to freedom from the devil** and their **only hope of being reunited with God.** Delusion is defined as a false belief or judgment about external reality that a person holds despite undeniable evidence to the contrary. These people chose to reject the Lord Jesus based on what they were taught by other non-believers without any validity and they never gave Him a chance in their lives. **As a result, they remain the devil's subjects**.

Others simply **ignored** or **rejected God's Gift of Salvation** in Christ and they never **took advantage of the 'Finished Works' of Christ on the Cross** and some **insisted on serving God their own way** *(their pagan religions)*. There are those who **chose to believe false doctrines** while others just **did not believe** that God is real; they all remain the devil's subjects.

You have those who **do not want to make any decision about God** and they drifted through life, some openly worship satan while many others chose to **worship the earth rather than the God who created it.** These are the ones that have made 'Climate Change' or 'Saving the Earth' and 'Depopulating the Earth' their new religion. Many of the world leaders who are still in rebellion to God's Word hound their citizens with these new doctrines from the pit of hell and out of them will rise the **devil's ultimate evil child known as the antichrist.**

Antichrist Rises to Fulfill the Devil's Desire

The rise of the evil World Leader will once and for all let man see what a union with the devil produces. As for the devil, he has been 'possessing people' and using them to defy God and His commandments ever since Adam chose his lies over God's Truth. He has been using people to **commit all sorts of wickedness** in order to **damn their souls. Until the**

coming of the Lord Jesus, man did not have the power to fight him and so, he kept humanity in bondage to him and sin. <u>The Lord Jesus defeated him on the Cross and in hell</u>. We see this recorded in **Colossians 2:15:**

> "And **having spoiled principalities and powers** *(defeated them)*, **he made a shew of them openly, triumphing over them in** *it* *(Jesus publicly disgraced the devil and his forces for all those in hell to see)*."

The Antichrist will Rule Over Those Who Chose the Devil

Concerning the **antichrist, the devil's ultimate desire is to fully indwell a person just as the Lord Jesus indwells all those who believe in Him.** The devil wants to rule over those who chose him. He wants to **exercise the full 'Adamic Authority' that he stole from Adam over all those on earth who rejected God and His Word and by default chose to follow him**. By not coming under the covering of the Lord Jesus *(the truth)*, the devil is the lord of these people as a result of his 'Adamic Authority' over them. **The devil wants to reign over them because they are his by default when they chose to hold onto the covenant that Adam made with him in the Garden of Eden.**

As a result, the rise of the antichrist is not about the devil but about God's honoring man's free will. What this means is that **God will honor the free will of those who chose the devil and He will allow the devil to indwell the antichrist so that he can lord it over them.** The man known as the antichrist or the Beast, is the vessel that the devil will use to accomplish his evil desires over all those who chose him! As a vessel that the devil indwells, the antichrist or the 'One World Leader' will unleash evil onslaught against all those on earth such as the world has never known before.

Although the antichrist will reign for 7 years, the last 42 months or 3½ years will be most brutal. Due to his wickedness and brutality, **people will cry for death and cannot find it because, God will allow them to reap the Fruit of their Union**

with the devil. This will finally prove to man once and for all that, a Union with the devil can only produce evil, chaos, wars, sufferings, gross wickedness and eternal damnation or separation from God.

This is why **at the end** of it all, **only those who allowed the Lord Jesus to free them** from the **union with the devil** and **bondage to sin, can qualify to live** in the 'New Earth' and the 'New Heaven' that He will reign over. Their union will be with God and God alone but **all those who chose the devil,** his evil ways and **rejected God's Word and Salvation,** would have been **thoroughly purged out of God's Creation.**

Nations Will Cry for the One World Leader; the Antichrist

The Bible says that **people in different nations** will demand or cry out for the leadership of the antichrist because of **wars, earthquakes, hardship, death, plagues, chaos, lawlessness** and all the turmoil going on all over the world. **Rather than cry out to God and His Son Jesus Christ,** there will be a cry from every nation for 'a world leader' that they think can **Save them.** They will 'wonder after him' or be fascinated with him. This means that a very **wicked man who is possessed by the devil will rise as the World Leader** and the Bible calls him **the antichrist.**

He will establish a '**One World Government**' and **rule with absolute evil and wickedness** for the last 3½ years of his 7-year reign. This is written in **Revelation 13:1-9**:

> "And I stood upon the sand of the sea, and **saw a beast rise up out of the sea,** having seven heads and ten horns, and **upon his horns ten crowns,** and upon his heads the name of blasphemy…and all the world wondered after the beast. 2 And the beast which I saw was like unto a **leopard,** and his feet were as the **feet of a bear,** and his mouth as the **mouth of a lion**: and the **dragon gave him his power,** and **his seat,** and **great authority.**

3 And I saw one of his heads as it were wounded to death; and his deadly wound was healed: and **all the world wondered after the beast**. 4 And **they worshipped the dragon** *(the devil)* **which gave power unto the beast**: and **they worshipped the beast**, saying, **Who is like unto the beast? who is able to make war with him?** 5 And **there was given unto him a mouth speaking great things and blasphemies**; and power was given unto him to continue forty and two months.

6 And he opened his mouth in blasphemy against God, to blaspheme his name, and his tabernacle, and them that dwell in heaven. 7 And **it was given unto him to make war with the saints, and to overcome them**: and power was given him over all kindreds, and tongues, and nations. 8 And **all that dwell upon the earth shall worship him, whose names are not written in the book of life** of the Lamb slain from the foundation of the world. 9 If any man have an ear, let him hear."

Be aware that **only those who rejected God** and His Son; the Lord Jesus Christ will worship the Beast; the antichrist. **He cannot forcefully place his Mark on people** but he will **forcefully coerce them to consent or die.** He will kill those who refuse but **for the sake of the eternal condition of your soul**, your job is to resist him and his forces no matter what.

What You Must Know about the Antichrist

He will initially pretend to be nice but will make a '7 Year Peace Treaty' with Israel and other nations according to **Daniel 9:27**:

"And he shall **confirm the covenant** with many for one week *(7 years)*: and in the midst of the week he shall cause the sacrifice and the oblation to cease, and for the overspreading of abominations he shall make it desolate, even until the consummation, and that determined shall be poured upon the desolate."

Halfway into the 7 year covenant, he will break it and will prevent the Jews from offering the newly restored daily sacrifices in the Temple that he helped them to build.

This is revealed in **Daniel 11:30-35**:

> "For the ships of Chittim shall come against him: **therefore he shall be grieved, and return, and have indignation against the holy covenant**: so shall he do; he shall even return, and have intelligence with them that forsake the holy covenant. *31* And arms shall stand on his part, and **they shall pollute the sanctuary of strength, and shall take away the daily sacrifice, and they shall place the abomination that maketh desolate**. *32* And such as do wickedly against the covenant shall he corrupt by flatteries: but the people that do know their God shall be strong, and do exploits.
>
> *33* And they that understand among the people shall instruct many: **yet they shall fall by the sword, and by flame, by captivity, and by spoil, many days**. *34* Now when they shall fall, they shall be holpen with a little help: but many shall cleave to them with flatteries. *35* And some of them of understanding shall fall, to try them, and to purge, and to make them white, even to the time of the end: because it is yet for a time appointed."

Also, after 3½ years of his 7 year rule, he will **show his true ugly side** as he begins to **persecute, hunt and kill Christians**; he will also **kill those who oppose his evil ways**. He will have a '**prophet**;' a **false prophet** that promotes him and his evil ways.

The Rise of the False Prophet

The **false prophet** will be the 'mouth-piece' of the **antichrist** who will use **deceptive acts** to **make fire come down from the sky**; a counterfeit demonic miracle in the presence of the **antichrist** and before **the world. He will set up an image of the antichrist or the Beast and he will command everyone**

on earth to worship the image of the Beast. God will allow him to have the ability to **make the image of the Beast speak** *(a demon will enter the image);* **commanding that all <u>those who refuse to worship it should be put to death</u>** just as King **Nebuchadnezzar** did with **his golden image** in Babylon.

Also, the **false prophet** will **decree that everyone receive either the <u>Mark</u>,** the **<u>name</u> of the Beast** or the **number of his name** which equals **666.** People will either receive this Mark on their **<u>Foreheads</u>** or in their **<u>Right Hand</u>** and those who **reject this Mark** will not be **able to <u>buy or sell</u>** anything including food.

The Lord Jesus made sure that He forewarned us about this false prophet because He did not want his **evil counterfeits or manifestations of false miracles** to take anyone by surprise. We read this in **Revelation 13:11-18:**

> "And I beheld **another beast** coming up **out of the earth; and he had <u>two horns</u>** *(authorities)* **<u>like a lamb</u>** *(was supposed to be a follower of Christ),* and **he spake as a dragon** *(the devil).* 12 And **he exerciseth all the power of the first beast before him,** and **causeth the earth and them which dwell <u>therein to worship the first beast</u>,** whose **deadly wound was healed** *(the beast survived an assassination attempt).*
>
> 13 And he **doeth great wonders,** so that **<u>he maketh fire come down from heaven on the earth in the sight of men</u>,** 14 And **<u>deceiveth them that dwell on the earth</u>** by the means of those miracles which he had power to do in the sight of the beast; **saying to them that dwell on the earth,** that **they should make an image to the beast,** which had the wound by a sword, and did live.
>
> 15 And **he had <u>power to give life unto the image of the beast</u>,** that **<u>the image of the beast should both speak</u>,** and cause **<u>that as many as would not worship the image of the beast should be killed</u>** *(no freedom to choose at this time).* 16 And he **causeth**

all, both **small** and **great**, **rich** and **poor**, **free** and **bond**, <u>**to receive a mark in their right hand,**</u> or **in their foreheads**:

17 And that <u>**no man might buy or sell, save he that had the mark,**</u> or the **name of the beast,** or **the number of his name**. *18* **Here is wisdom**. Let him that hath understanding count the number of the beast: **for it is the number of a man**; and his number is **Six hundred threescore and six (666)**."

No Free Will Under the Antichrist and the False Prophet

We are now grounded in the knowledge that when God created Adam *(Man)* from whom all humanity descended, He gave him a **free will; meaning the** <u>**freedom to choose**</u> *(good and not evil)* so that, Adam can **effectively exercise dominion** over everything on earth. **God Himself** <u>**honors this free will in every human and He does not override it.**</u> It is the reason why He does not force anyone to believe in Christ; it is a matter of an individual's choice. He once told me that, "**A person has the right to choose hell if that is what the person wants!**"

This <u>**God-given right to choose while on earth**</u> is called the '**Basic Human Rights**' all over the world. For example, the **United States Constitution** recognizes this **free will** or **freedom** as certain '**Unalienable Rights**' from **God the Creator** as it states:

"We hold these truths to be self-evident, that **all men are created equal, that they are** <u>**endowed by their Creator**</u> *(God)* with certain **unalienable rights**, that among these are Life, Liberty and the pursuit of Happiness."

Unalienable rights means that you cannot separate a person from these God-given rights. This is why the founders of the United States made sure that these rights are guaranteed by the US Constitution. It is why those who are fed up with tyranny and oppressive governments all over the world, run to United States; the land of the free. It is because of this free will that people naturally get angry when someone tries to **force, mandate** or **make them do something they do not want to do.** Even a baby will push the bottle out of his or her mouth when it does not want it; we are all born with this free will.

Unfortunately, **under the reign of the antichrist and his false prophet,** the scripture in Revelation 13 you just read tells us that, if you were left behind and are now under them, **the freedom to choose or reject the Mark or the name of the Beast will not be available to you!** Freedom of choice is not one of the devil's attributes so, **free will is going to be trampled** by the **antichrist** and **people will be mandated to take his Mark or the number of his name or die by beheading.** The **devil who indwells the antichrist or the Beast** does not offer any choice, freedom or love. He is the opposite of Christ and of everything that is good.

What You Should Know about the Mark of the Beast

By accepting the **Mark of the Beast, you are pledging your soul to the devil forever** and **you cannot revoke your decision to accept the Mark** because the devil will not let you; he owns you at this point. God makes it clear in **Revelation 19:20** that all those who received the Mark will be **cast by God into the Lake of Fire with the antichrist and the false prophet.** Therefore whatever the cost, do not accept the Mark; instead, let them kill you:

> "And **the beast was taken,** and **with him the false prophet** that **wrought miracles before him,** with **which he deceived them that had received the mark of the beast,** and **them that worshipped his image.** These both **were cast alive into a lake of fire burning with brimstone."**

Again, the **Mark of the Beast** cannot be **forcefully placed on you** but **they will kill you when you reject it.** Meaning that **you will be coerced to accept it or be beheaded** but by accepting the

Mark under this duress or fear of physical death, **you will be telling God that because of your fear of physical death, you choose satan over Him forever.** Therefore, you leave Him no room but to **condemn you with satan, his forces and all those who aligned themselves with them.** As a result:

1. You will **forever spend eternity** in the **Lake of Fire** being **tormented**
2. You will be **forever separated from God** and **everything that is good; you will never know anything good again**
3. You will **only know pain** and **anguish** but **you cannot die** or **get relief** from your **torment**

Therefore, think about all these damnable consequences and please, **reject the Mark**. Again, know that even if you are killed *(beheaded)* by the **forces of the antichrist for choosing to believe in the Lord Jesus, you will go straight to Heaven and be rewarded by God with eternal life**. This is written in **Revelation 12:11** about those who were killed for their faith in Christ; they walked in victory into Glory because they are overcomers.

> "And **they** <u>**overcame him by the blood of the Lamb,**</u> and by the <u>**word of their testimony**</u> *(their confession of faith in Christ);* and **they loved** <u>**not their lives unto the death**</u> *(they were not afraid to die for Christ)."*

Remember that the Lord Jesus laid down His Life for you and He was greatly rewarded by God as recorded in **Philippians 2:5-11:**

> "Let this mind be in you, which was also in Christ Jesus: 6 Who, being in the form of God, thought it not robbery to be equal with God: 7 But **made himself of no reputation, and took upon him the form of a servant, and was made in the likeness of men:** 8 And being found in fashion <u>**as a man, he humbled himself,**</u> and <u>**became obedient unto death, even the death of the cross.**</u>

9 Wherefore God also hath highly exalted him, and given him a name which is above every name: *10* That at the name of Jesus every knee should bow, of things in heaven, and things in earth, and things under the earth; *11* And that every tongue should confess that Jesus Christ is Lord, to the glory of God the Father."

This should **inspire you to <u>lay your life down for Him</u> with the <u>knowledge that God will also greatly reward you</u>**. I advise you to read the *Chapter titled: Be Prepared for Martyrdom* in this book, you will have a more detailed understanding of why God requires martyrdom from the Tribulation Saints. I am by no means saying that it will be easy but with God on your side, **"you can do all things;"** including **<u>laying down your life for Christ</u>.**

Chapter 9
There will be a 'One World Religion'

Vulnerability of Those Practicing other Religions

After Rapture, a lot of people who were practicing **Islam, Hinduism, Buddhism, Shintoism, Communism, Paganism, Satanism, New Age, Occultism** of all sorts, **Atheism** or 'Free-thinkers'** are <u>wondering where their religious beliefs have left them</u>. A lot of these people are now **changing their beliefs** right after **faithful Christians and the innocent children** all over the world disappeared regardless of the religions of their parents. Some of them saw their babies disappear before their eyes and there was nothing they could do about it.

Many of those who previously claimed that they were not '**bound by religion**' or were 'not religious,' are now wondering about what their fate will be as they want to know the truth about what happened. Again, the answer is very simple: **the Lord Jesus came and took the Christians who believed in Him and who walked faithfully according to His will! He also took all the innocent children all over the world.**

A lot of these people who still choose to hold on to their erroneous beliefs *(choose the bondage of their wrong religions)* even after Rapture, will be **blinded by the devil** so that they will believe all the lies being fed to them by the antichrist. As a result, many of them will <u>believe the lies</u> from the antichrist that the **Rapture never truly happened.**

The Worship of the Antichrist and 'One World Religion'

Along with the '**One World Religion**' that will be instituted as the antichrist gains power, he will desire to be worshiped. He will accomplish this with the help of the **false prophet** as revealed in **Revelation 13:4-16:**

> "And **they worshipped the dragon which gave power unto the beast: and they worshipped the beast**, saying, Who is like unto the beast? who is able to make war with him?... *12* And he

exerciseth all the power of the first beast before him, and causeth the earth and them which dwell therein to worship the first beast, whose deadly wound was healed.

13 And **he doeth great wonders, so that he maketh fire come down from heaven on the earth in the sight of men,** 14 And **deceiveth them that dwell on the earth by the means of those miracles which he had power to do in the sight of the beast; saying to them that dwell on the earth, that they should make an image to the beast,** which had the wound by a sword, and did live.

15 And **he had power to give life unto the image of the beast, that the image of the beast should both speak, and cause that as many as would not worship the image of the beast should be killed.** 16 And he causeth all, both small and great, rich and poor, free and bond, to receive a mark in their right hand, or in their foreheads."

We learned that **he will not regard the Almighty God that made the Heaven and earth;** meaning that it is already foretold that <u>**the antichrist will go after a strange god**</u>. I believe that the antichrist will endorse Islam over Christianity and 'preach climate change.' We are told about his adoption of a non-Christian religion in **Daniel 11:37-39:**

> "**Neither shall he regard the God of his fathers** *(Judeo-Christian God)*, nor the desire of women, nor regard any god: for he shall magnify himself above all. 38 **But in his estate shall he honour the God of forces:** and <u>**a god whom his fathers knew not shall he honour**</u> **with gold, and silver, and with precious stones, and pleasant things.**
>
> 39 Thus shall he do in the most strongholds with **a strange god, whom he shall acknowledge and increase with glory:** and he shall cause

them to rule over many *(at this time, watch out for the Muslims)*, and **shall divide the land** *(Israel; Jerusalem)* **for gain."**

The Antichrist Will Persecute the Jews

After building a Temple in Jerusalem for the Jews, many of them will initially follow the antichrist but when **he takes a seat in the Temple and declares himself to be the Almighty God, the Jews will reject him.** The Jews will finally see him for who he is; a liar! **Therefore, he will hate them and seek to kill them for <u>rejecting him</u>.** The antichrist declaring himself to be god is recorded in **2 Thessalonians 2:4-10:**

> "Who **opposeth and exalteth himself above all that is called God, or that is worshipped**; so that he **as God sitteth in the temple of God, shewing himself that he is God**... 8 And **then shall that Wicked be revealed,** whom the Lord shall consume with the spirit of his mouth, and shall destroy with the brightness of his coming: 9 **Even him, whose coming is after the working of Satan** with **all power and signs and lying wonders,** 10 And with all **deceivableness of unrighteousness in them that perish; because <u>they received not the love of the truth</u>, that they might be saved."**

Both the **Jews and the Christians will form the core of the group that the antichrist will seek to kill because they chose to worship and trust the God that created the Heaven and earth.** Yes, the God that owns all souls.

He Will Unite all Religions in the World Under One Umbrella

Those <u>still practicing their pagan religions</u> after **Rapture occurred** will be **deceived** by the **antichrist** to <u>combine their religions</u> under '**One Brotherhood of Mankind**' in order to bring about peace on earth. Therefore, he will call for the <u>different religious faiths</u> **to come together because they are**

all on the 'same path' to God. This will be one of the devil's last ultimate deceptions.

Therefore, make no mistake about it, **besides demanding to be worshipped** as god, the **antichrist** will **unite all the world's pagan religions** under **one umbrella** and nations will yield to his plans. **Even before Rapture, the globalist and major world leaders including the Pope** were already laying the foundation to unite all the religions of the world to achieve '**World Peace.**' They preached that **wars** and **global conflicts are the results of opposing world religions** and therefore they need to be consolidated.

To achieve this, there have been discussions, meetings and conferences for Judaism, Christianity, Islam, Hinduism, Buddhism, Satanism, Occultism, Atheism, Agnosticism, etc., to come together under **one religious umbrella** in order to **create Peace and Security**! In 2021 they began constructing a building in **Germany** that they call, '**The House of One**' and with locations in other countries to **house all the religions**. For years before Rapture, some Catholics and Islamic groups have been **coming together in worship** and they call it **Chrislam!** Do not be surprised if this is amplified in the days you now find yourself. The antichrist will turn all those who are under his '**One World Religion**' against the Christians **and the Jews**! He will declare them to be the enemies of peace.

Many people will buy into the deceptions of the antichrist but **you will do well to avoid them** because our God does not "**co-mingle**" with other gods. In fact, He said this in **Isaiah 42:8:**

> "I am the LORD: that is my name: and **my glory will I not give to another**, neither my praise to graven images."

And in **Isaiah 43:10-11**, he said:

> "Ye are my witnesses, saith the LORD, and my servant whom I have chosen: that ye may know and believe me, and understand **that I am he: before me there was no God formed, neither**

shall there be after me. *11* I, even I, am the LORD; and beside me there is no saviour."

The Pope as the False Prophet

Be aware that the **Pope** of the **Roman Catholic Church** will be the very **mouth-piece of the antichrist** and he will serve as his '**false prophet.**' At this point, you need to read again, the scripture which says that the false prophet will **command all humanity to worship the Beast** *(the antichrist)*, and to take his Mark. He will also **command that all those who refused the Mark be killed**. The scripture in **Revelation 13:11-17** is worth repeating here for emphasis of who the Pope is:

"And I beheld another beast coming up out of the earth; and he had **two horns like a lamb** *(Apostate Christian and head of the Roman Catholic Church)*, and **he spake as a dragon** *(like the devil)*. *12* And **he exerciseth all the power of the first beast before him, and causeth the earth and them which dwell therein to worship the first beast**, whose deadly wound was healed.

13 And **he doeth great wonders, so that he maketh fire come down from heaven on the earth in the sight of men,** *14* **And deceiveth them that dwell on the earth by the means of those miracles which he had power to do in the sight of the beast; saying to them that dwell on the earth, that they should make an image to the beast,** which had the wound by a sword, and did live.

15 And **he had power to give life unto the image of the beast, that the image of the beast should both speak, and cause that as many as would not worship the image of the beast should be killed.** *16* **And he causeth all, both small and great, rich and poor, free and bond, to receive a mark in their right hand, or in their foreheads:** *17*

And **that no man might buy or sell, save he that
had the mark, or the name of the beast, or the
number of his name.**"

Why is the False Prophet Portrayed in Scripture as a Lamb?

The Lord Jesus told the **Apostle Peter** in **John 21:15**, "**Feed
my Lambs.**" The Pope who claims to sit on **Peter's Seat in the
church** is supposed to be the **Lord's lamb** but he will make
himself the "**Servant of Sin**" to the antichrist. As you just saw
in the above scripture, he will serve as the agent or 'mouth-
piece' of the Beast *(the antichrist)*. **This is why if you are
currently in the Roman Catholic Church, get out of it before
it is too late.** Be sure to read the chapter titled, *Flee from the
Roman Catholic Church* in just a few chapters below.

Do not Worship the Beast or Listen to the False Prophet

Know that **all those who listen to the false prophet** *(the
Pope)* and **worship the Beast** called the antichrist **will be
judged and punished** by God. Again, they will be tormented
in the **Lake of Fire** forever — **Revelation 14:9-11:**

> "And the third angel followed them, saying with
> a loud voice, **If any man worship the beast and
> his image, and receive his mark in his forehead,
> or in his hand,** 10 **The same shall drink of the
> wine of the wrath of God, which is poured out
> without mixture into the cup of his indignation;**
>
> and he shall be tormented with fire and brimstone
> in the presence of the holy angels, and in the
> presence of the **Lamb:** 11 And the **smoke of their
> torment ascendeth up forever and ever:** and <u>they
> have no rest day nor night</u>, <u>who worship the
> beast and his image, and whosoever receiveth
> the mark of his name.</u>"

As you can see, **it is better to suffer and die for Christ on
earth than to burn in an Eternal Fire.**

Chapter 10
Be Prepared for Martyrdom

Definition of a Martyr

A Martyr is a person who is killed because of their religious beliefs. Therefore, when God calls you to be a martyr, it means that God requires you to be willing to die for the sake of Jesus Christ and His Gospel. It is the hardest and most difficult thing that God requires from His Children.

Most Christians do not Know of Their Martyrdom Call

A lot of **Christians are not aware that God has called them to be martyrs until the <u>very moment</u> they are <u>being killed</u>.** Therefore, every believer must be aware that being martyred is part of our Christian calling. Two good examples are the disciple called **Stephen** and the **Apostle James**; the brother of John the beloved — **Acts 12:1-2:**

> "Now about that time **Herod the king stretched forth his hands to vex certain of the church.** 2 And **he killed James the brother of John with the sword."**

Apart from the **Apostle John** whom the Romans could not kill; even after **boiling him in hot oil, all the other disciples were martyred.** Again, **Christians who are martyred were not aware of this 'call of martyrdom' until the very moment they are being killed.**

Tribulation Saints Duration of Martyrdom Process

Laying down one's life is not an easy thing to do because **the human soul does not want to die. Your martyrdom process will be quick *(beheading)* but you will step right into Glory and the Lord will be with you for the entire process.** Remind yourself that it will only take a few minutes. This should give you some comfort because as you are going to read below, the Lord's martyrdom process was 6 hours long with prolonged pain.

The Lord's Painful Prolonged Martyrdom Process

In the case of our Lord Jesus Christ in the Garden of Gethsemane, **He told the disciples that <u>His soul was exceedingly sorrowful unto death</u>** as **He struggled to lay down His personal will** and **surrender to the Father's will** which was for Him to go to the Cross for us — **Matthew 26:38-44:**

> "Then saith he unto them, **My soul is exceeding sorrowful, even unto death**: tarry ye here, and watch with me. 39 And he went a little further, and **fell on his face, and prayed, saying, O my Father, if it be possible, let this cup pass from me**: nevertheless **not as I will, but as thou wilt**...
>
> 42 He went away again the second time, and prayed, saying, **O my Father, if this cup may not pass away from me, except I drink it, thy will be done.** 43 And he came and found them asleep again: for their eyes were heavy. 44 And **he left them, and went away again, and prayed the third time, saying the same words.**"

The Lord prayed three times for His assignment on the Cross (*the Cup*) **to pass from Him but each time, He surrendered to the Father's will.** For the Lord, not only was He going to be **publicly humiliated, mocked, spat on, have a wicked crown of thorns placed on His head, He was also going to have 5–7" nails driven into His hands and feet before dying a very slow, painful and suffocating death on the Cross.**

One can only guess that the Lord would have been fine with going through all the sufferings for us but **to make matters worse for Him, the Holy Spirit will depart from Him!** This is the **terror of every Spirit-filled Christian**; losing the Holy Spirit. It is why King David cried in fear in **Psalm 51:11:**

> "Cast me not away from thy presence; and **take not thy holy spirit from me.**"

Losing the Presence and Union with God the Father and the Holy Spirit was the reason the Lord Jesus sweated blood because the **devil and all the demons in hell were coming** after Him and the <u>Spirit of God the Father that has been with Him from Eternity, will for the first time depart from Him</u>; He will be apart from God the Father! He had never experienced this in all His existence. This is why **Luke 22:44 says:**

> "And being in an agony he prayed more earnestly: and **his sweat was as it were great drops of blood falling down to the ground.**"

Just think about it, the one time that the Lord will really need God the Father and the Holy Spirit, they will not be there with Him; this was a **spiritual terror of the highest degree. Christ being the 'Last Adam,'** God the Father <u>needed for Him to go through the process of suffering and death on the Cross as a regular man because the first Adam was a regular man</u> when the devil stole his authority over the earth.

Therefore, the Lord Jesus had to be <u>a regular man</u> to confront, defeat the devil, death and hell in order to get <u>the 'Adamic Authority' back from the devil for us</u>. A man *(Adam)* lost the authority over earth to the devil *(not 'God')* so a man *(Christ, the Last Adam)* was required to take it back from the devil. **All this happened because Adam made a 'spiritual legal transaction' with the devil and our God who is righteous and just honored it;** He respected Adam's freewill. In Him, there is no darkness; He is fair to all His creation.

This should encourage **Tribulation Saints** because the Lord will be with them in all that they will go through. He knows the terror of not having the Holy Spirit when you are confronting evil. As a result, He will make sure to be with them and to guide them as He promised in **Matthew 28:20:**

> "…And, lo, <u>I am with you alway, even unto the end of the world</u>. Amen."

And in **Hebrews 13:5:**

> "…For he hath said, **I will never leave thee, nor forsake thee.**"

And **Deuteronomy 31:6** says:

> "Be strong and of a good courage, fear not, nor be afraid of them: for the Lord thy God, he it

is that doth go with thee; **he will not fail thee, nor forsake thee."**

Those Martyred During the Great Tribulation are Blessed

We read about the blessings that await all those who will be martyred during the **Great Tribulation** period in **Revelation 14:12-13**. **God will not forget the price they paid for the sake of the Gospel or the works that they did during this time:**

> **"Here is the patience of the saints** *(those at the time of tribulation):* **here are they that keep the commandments of God, and the faith of Jesus.**
> 13 And I heard a voice from heaven saying unto me, Write, **Blessed are the dead which die in the Lord from henceforth** *(during the Tribulation):* **Yea, saith the Spirit, that they may rest from their labours; and** <u>their works do follow them."</u>

They will be greatly rewarded by God in Heaven. Although, they might be killed physically, **the Lord calls them overcomers of the devil in Revelation 12:11:**

> "And **they** *(Tribulations Saints)* **overcame him by the blood of the Lamb, and by the word of their testimony;** and **they loved not their lives unto the death** *(meaning spare their lives on earth)."*

They did not value their lives so much that they traded it for a temporary escape from the pain of physical death on earth. Instead, they valued spending Eternity with God in Heaven rather than be burnt in hell forever after God's Judgment. According to the Word of God in **Revelation 15:2-4**, we see <u>martyred Tribulation Saints</u> rejoicing and praising God in Heaven:

> "And I saw as it were a sea of glass mingled with fire: and **them** *(Tribulation Saints)* <u>that had gotten the victory over the beast, and over his image, and over his mark, and over the number of his name</u>, stand on the sea of glass *(in Heaven)*, **having the harps of God.**

3 And **they sing the song of Moses the servant of God, and the song of the Lamb, saying, Great and marvellous are thy works, Lord God Almighty; just and true are thy ways, thou king of saints.** 4 **Who shall not fear thee, O Lord, and glorify thy name? for thou only art holy**: for all nations shall come and worship before thee; **for thy judgments are made manifest."**

Do you now see from the scripture above that **you will not perish when you hold on to your faith in Christ** even if you are beheaded during the Great Tribulation period? This should encourage you greatly.

The Lord Forewarned Us about Martyrdom for His Sake

The Lord **forewarned** us all about being martyred for His sake in **Matthew 24:9.** It is something every Christian should now be aware of; **especially these days of the Great Tribulation:**

"Then shall they **deliver you up** to be **afflicted,** and **shall kill you**: and <u>ye shall be hated of all nations for my name's sake."</u>

And in **John 16:2**, He said:

"…Yea, **the time cometh,** that <u>whoso-ever killeth you will think that he doeth God service</u>."

But in **Matthew 10:28,** He told us **not to fear human killers** because, **they can only kill the human body** but **they cannot touch your <u>Spirit</u> or your <u>Soul</u>:**

"And **fear not them which kill the body, but are not able to kill the soul**: but rather fear him *(God)* which is able to destroy both soul and body in hell."

As a Christian, you cannot tell when you are going to be in a place where you will be persecuted or killed for your Christian faith. Therefore, **all Tribulation Saints must be ready at all times for martyrdom.** Even before Rapture occurred, Christians were being targeted and killed in different places all over the world because of their faith in Jesus Christ. I cannot even imagine what will be happening during the time of tribulation.

The Lord Jesus Knew that He was Born to be Martyred

The Lord Jesus was born where **Lambs meant to be sacrificed are born and kept** — a stable! Throughout His life on earth, He was **aware that He was born to die for our sins** and He said it in **Mark 10:33-45:**

> "...Behold, we go up to Jerusalem; and **the Son of man shall be delivered unto the chief priests,** and **unto the scribes;** and <u>**they shall condemn him to death,**</u> and **shall deliver him to the Gentiles:** *34* And they shall mock him, and shall scourge him, and shall spit upon him, and **shall kill him**: and the third day he shall rise again... *45* For even the Son of man came not to be ministered unto, but to minister, and <u>**to give his life a ransom for many**</u>."

Again, the **Prophet Isaiah foretold** this about Christ dying for our sin in **Isaiah 53:4-10** some 500 years before He was born and that God the Father will sacrifice Him on the Cross for our sins:

> "**Surely he hath borne our griefs, and carried our sorrows**: yet we did esteem him stricken, smitten of God, and afflicted. *5* **But he was wounded for our transgressions, he was bruised for our iniquities: the chastisement of our peace was upon him; and with his stripes we are healed.** *6* <u>**All we like sheep have gone astray;**</u> we have <u>**turned everyone to his own way;**</u> and <u>**the LORD hath laid on him the iniquity of us all.**</u>
>
> *7* **He was oppressed, and he was afflicted, yet he opened not his mouth: he is brought as a lamb to the slaughter,** and **as a sheep before her shearers is dumb, so he openeth not his mouth.** *8* **He was taken from prison and from judgment:** and who shall declare his generation? <u>**for he was cut off out**</u>

of the land of the living: for the transgression of my people was he stricken.

9 And he made his grave with the wicked, and with the rich in his death; because he had done no violence, **neither was any deceit in his mouth.** 10 Yet **it pleased the LORD to bruise** him; **he hath put him to grief: when thou shalt make His soul an offering for sin, He shall see His seed** *(faithful Christians),* he shall **prolong** his days *(they will tell others about Him),* and the pleasure of the LORD shall prosper in his hand."

Some Early Saints Knew They were Called to be Martyrs

There are those who **already know** that **God has called them** to **lay down their lives** for **the Kingdom**; they are not afraid to be killed for Christ. There is a certain **'Freedom'** in **knowing that you will one day lay down your life for Christ because you stop being afraid of man and trust in God that when the hour comes, He will take the sting of death for you.**

The **Apostle Peter** is an example of those called to be martyrs and the Lord Jesus told him this personally as we see in **John 21:18-19:**

> "Verily, verily, I say unto thee *(Peter),* When thou wast young, thou girdedst thyself, and walkedst whither thou wouldest: **but when thou shalt be old, thou shalt stretch forth thy hands, and another shall gird thee, and carry thee whither thou wouldest not.** 19 **This spake** he, **signifying by what death he should glorify God**. And when he had spoken this, he saith unto him, Follow me."

Just as the Lord said, Peter was crucified upside down on a cross in Rome in the very spot where the Vatican is now located. A prophet called Agabus also told the Apostle Paul about what awaited him in Jerusalem as written in **Acts 21:10-14.** He was essentially telling Paul what will be the beginning of his journey toward martyrdom:

"And as we tarried there many days, there came down from Judaea a certain prophet, named Agabus. *11* And when he was come unto us, he took Paul's girdle, and bound his own hands and feet, and said, **Thus saith the Holy Ghost, So shall the Jews at Jerusalem bind the man that owneth this girdle, and shall deliver him into the hands of the Gentiles.**

12 And when we heard these things, both we, and they of that place, besought him not to go up to Jerusalem. *13* **Then Paul answered, What mean ye to weep and to break mine heart? for I am ready not to be bound only, but also to die at Jerusalem for the name of the Lord Jesus.** *14* And when he would not be persuaded, we ceased, saying, The will of the Lord be done."

The Lord Jesus also told Paul that he was to go to Rome be a witness for Him; there, he was **martyred** by the emperor Nero.

All Tribulation Saints are Now Called to be Martyrs

As a Believer in the days of Great Tribulation, it may seem that the only way to keep your faith in Christ is martyrdom. It is the 'hard way' to make it to Heaven because most people failed to choose the 'easy way;' making Christ your Lord before Rapture occurred. Do not lose hope because through it all, the Lord will be there with you whether you see Him in a vision or not as you are taking your last steps.

My Vision of a Christian Being Beheaded

*I can personally **attest to the truth that the Lord is with all His martyrs** because of what He showed me in a vision some years ago when a radical Islamic group kidnapped two business men during their reign of terror in Iraq. **In this vision, they had beheaded the first man who was not a Christian but when they grabbed the second man who was a Christian, <u>the Holy Spirit showed up</u>.***

122

The man had no idea that the Holy Spirit was there with him *and I watched as this very terrified man's neck was being lined up on one of the concrete steps of the stairway. Right before the Islamic terrorist raised his machete, the Holy Spirit lined the step underneath the man's neck with a pure white cloth.*

When they cut the man's neck, the Holy Spirit made sure He collected all his blood; even the ones that had splattered! I watched as the Holy Spirit made sure that not a drop of this Christian's blood was left behind!

Therefore, **when you are faced with the forces of the antichrist who want to cut off your head,** call on the Lord to be with you just as He was also with the beheaded man in Iraq and the disciple called Stephen; it is your hour of need. He saw the evil forces coming for you before you did and He will do for you what He did for Stephen — **Acts 7:54-60:**

> "When they heard these things, they were cut to the heart, and they gnashed on him with their teeth. 55 But he *(Stephen)*, **being full of the Holy Ghost, looked up stedfastly into heaven, and saw the glory of God, and Jesus standing on the right hand of God,** 56 And said, Behold, I see the heavens opened, and the Son of man standing on the right hand of God.
>
> 57 Then they cried out with a loud voice, and stopped their ears, and ran upon him with one accord, 58 **And cast him out of the city, and stoned him:** and the witnesses laid down their clothes at a young man's feet, whose name was Saul. 59 **And they stoned Stephen, <u>calling upon God, and saying, Lord Jesus, receive my spirit.</u>** 60 And **he** *(Stephen)* **<u>kneeled down, and cried with a loud voice, Lord, lay not this sin to their charge</u>. And when he had said this, <u>he fell asleep</u>** *(died)*."

Know that **God has great reward for you when you refuse the Mark of the Beast and hold on to your faith in Christ —** **Revelation 20:4:**

> "And I saw thrones, and they sat upon them, and judgment was given unto them: and **I saw the souls of them that were** <u>beheaded</u> **for the witness of Jesus, and for the word of God, and which had not worshipped the beast, neither his image, neither had received his mark upon their foreheads, or in their hands;** and <u>they lived and reigned with Christ a thousand years</u>."

This is why <u>you should not give up</u> because it is not over for you after **missing Rapture. The Lord Jesus in His Wisdom made plans for you to join Him even after Rapture.**

Questions Facing You Now:

1. Are you **willing to lay down your life for Christ** and His Gospel?
2. When **faced with the choice of death** for your faith, what will you do?
3. When **offered rejecting Jesus to spare yourself** from being killed *(a temporary relief)*, will you **stand firm in your faith in Him**?
4. Will you **choose Him no matter what**?
5. **What price are you willing to pay for Christ** who laid down His life for you?

What will be Your Response?

You must **already have a 'prepared answer' to these questions** because you just might come face-to-face with it soon. For example, your hiding place might be discovered by the forces of the antichrist and some of your so-called friends, false brethren or family members might betray you. You might walk out the door and never make it back home.

Again, most people **do not know that God called them to lay down their lives for Christ but during the Tribulation period, <u>the Bible says that many of those left behind will be</u>**

martyred. Therefore, you must be prepared beforehand and **walk as if each day is your last on earth**.

Accept the Call of Martyrdom

You should purpose before-hand to **accept God's call of martyrdom** upon your life as a Tribulation Saint. It will help you to simplify your life in the days that you are now living and you will not be living in fear of what man can do to you but in the **Liberty that is in Christ Jesus knowing that when you put off your earthly tabernacle** *(your body)*, **you will put on a heavenly one.** Every Believer in Christ will be given a new body — **2 Corinthians 5:1-9:**

> **"For we know that if our earthly house of this tabernacle** *(body)* **were dissolved, we have a building of God** *(a new body)*, **an house not made with hands, Eternal in the heavens.** 2 For in this we groan, earnestly desiring to be clothed upon with our house which is from heaven...
>
> 6 Therefore **we are always confident, knowing that, whilst we are at home in the body, we are absent from the Lord:** 7 (For we walk by faith, not by sight:) 8 We are confident, I say, and **willing rather to be absent from the body** *(to die)*, **and to be present with the Lord.** 9 Wherefore we labour, that, whether present or absent, we may be accepted of him."

Emotions Tribulation Martyrs Might go Through

1. **Sorrow** - As you accept the call of martyrdom and are coming face-to-face with its reality, you will go through some emotional phases. You might feel very **sorrowful**; after all, **no one wants to die especially by beheading.** No human soul wants death because dying was not part of God's plan for man.

   As we read earlier in this chapter, even **the Lord Jesus prayed and asked God the Father to let the "Cup Pass from Him"** but His Father said, **no.** Instead, **God sent angels to strengthen Him** and He gave Him the **Grace that**

He needed for what He must do on the Cross. Again, you too can **ask God for grace in the Name of Lord Jesus.** You can also tell God that, **"Not your will but His be done."** Doing this will help you release your life to God and He will not let you down; even if you are killed physically.

2. **Fear - Another emotion that you must overcome is Fear itself.** The Fear of pain and the agony that will be involved in beheading; the **fear of the process of your death and its duration** is something you have to commit to the Lord. Keep reminding yourself that God has not given you the spirit of fear — **2 Timothy 1:7-8:**

> **"For God hath not given us the spirit of fear; but of power, and of love, and of a sound mind.** *8* **Be not thou therefore ashamed of the testimony of our Lord,** nor of me his prisoner: but **be thou partaker of the afflictions of the gospel according to the power of God..."**

Now you must hold on to Christ no matter what. He is your life and your eternity.

3. **Grief** - Do not let **grief overcome you** but know that the Lord will be with you through all that will happen in your life. The Bible says in **Romans 14:7-8** that we belong to the Lord whether we live or die:

> "For none of us liveth to himself, and no man dieth to himself. *8* **For whether we live, we live unto the Lord;** and **whether we die, we die unto the Lord:** <u>whether we live therefore, or die, we are the Lord's.</u>"

Be a Witness of God's Word

As you have been reading throughout this book, **all those who have their earthly bodies destroyed** *(through beheading)* **will receive a heavenly one. They will come back with the Lord Jesus Christ when He returns to destroy the New World leader** *(the Beast)* **7 years after Rapture.** By now, you know that the **Bible is the accurate Word of God** and that **whatever**

it says will happen in the future, will surely happen as it is written. God's Word in the Bible cannot return to God without carrying out what God sent it to do.

Just think about it, right now in Heaven, millions of people who were taken in Rapture are watching **you on earth reading what God's Son; the Lord Jesus Christ instructed me to tell you before Rapture occurred!** If you have read the Bible, the events in your world testify that the things that you read are coming to pass. This book is based on what is written in the Bible which you can now be a witness of and share with others that the Bible is true.

Obey the Lord's Word in **Mark 16:15-16** to preach the Gospel:

> "And he said unto them, **Go ye into all the world, and preach the gospel to every creature.** *16* He that believeth and is baptized shall be saved; but he that believeth not shall be damned."

Fellowship with Those Who Have Embraced their Call of Martyrdom

Fellowship with like-minded Believers will encourage you in the days you are in so, seek them out if possible but beware of traitors — **wolves in sheep's clothing**. You all can hide together while you conduct **prayer meetings, Bible studies** as well as **Praise and Worship** but be careful to avoid those who will seek to betray you.

God's Purpose for Requiring Martyrdom

You must know that nothing takes God by surprise; He declares the end from the beginning *(Isaiah 46:10)*. He ordained for the death of martyrs to glorify Him from the very beginning. **Therefore, being martyred is for the glory of God.** It means that **God wants you to use the <u>last few minutes of your life as a testimony that He sent His children to tell the world that He loves them</u>** (John 3:16-17) **but in response, <u>the world mistreated and killed them</u>**.

The killing of God's children including the Tribulation Saints and previous martyrs, will without doubt **let the world know why God had to condemn them to hell.** None of the people of the world will have any excuse before God when He lets them know of their fate in hell. **God the Father once told me concerning satan, "I will show him how much he must suffer for what he has done to my children;"** meaning Christians. The same will go for all the devil's children *(the wicked people)* who helped satan to kill Christians!

Summary of the Benefits of Being a Martyr

1. You get to fulfill what the Apostle Paul desired and cried for in **Philippians 3:10-11** which was to know the **Power of Christ's Resurrection:**

   "That <u>I may know him,</u> and **the power of his resurrection,** and **the fellowship of his sufferings, being made conformable unto his death;** 11 <u>If by any means I might attain unto the resurrection of the dead.</u>"

2. You will qualify to live in the **'City of Martyrs'** in **Heaven;** only martyrs live there

3. **Martyrs are the most respected Believers in Heaven**

4. You will experience the **'Peace of the Martyrdom Call'** — fearing no man

5. Once **you accept your call,** you find that you no longer:
   - Worry about dying before your **time or in another manner of death**
   - Worry about dying in a **car or plane crash**
   - **Assurance that the Lord will be with you** through the process
   - Your death will **glorify God** for all of Eternity
   - Your death does not mean that the devil has won but that he is going to the **Lake of Fire** while **you are Heaven bound!**

Words of Encouragement

1. Do not dwell on the call but be focused on living your life knowing that **martyrdom is only going to be the, *"last few minutes of your life"***

2. God does not want you to spend the next years of your life worrying about the **last few minutes of it**

3. Ask the Lord to let you know when you have **'Finished your Assignment'** on earth even during the Tribulation; **you are only on earth to finish your assignment**

4. Again, ask for grace and help for the <u>**hour of your Exit**</u>

5. Constantly remind yourself that many Christians will not qualify to dwell in the **'City of Martyrs,'** but **when you get to Heaven, you will qualify to dwell in it**

6. I say to you again, settle it in your heart that you **will lay down your life for Christ** when the occasion arises — **Philippians 1:21-29:**

   > "For to me to live is Christ, and to die is gain...*29* For unto you it is given in the behalf of Christ, **not only to believe on him, but also to suffer for his sake.**"

7. **Do not choose the Mark of the Beast to save your physical life;** those who do will go into eternal damnation. Remember the Lord's warning in **Luke 14:26-30:**

   > "If any man come to me, and hate not his father, and mother, and wife, and children, and brethren, and sisters, yea, <u>**and his own life also, he cannot be my disciple**</u>. *27* And **whosoever doth not bear his cross, and come after me, cannot be my disciple.**
   >
   > *28* For which of you, intending to **build a tower, sitteth not down first, and counteth the cost, whether he have sufficient to finish it?** *29* Lest haply, after he hath laid the foundation, and is not able to finish it, all that behold it begin to mock him, *30* Saying, **This man began to build, and was not able to finish.**"

   Be prepared to endure whatever comes your way to the end; even martyrdom. It is called **'Counting the Cost'** and being willing to pay it.

The Lord Jesus's Call to "Follow Me"

When it **comes to martyrdom, the Lord Jesus' call to, "Follow Me" takes on a higher level** of demand and meaning for the Christians. This is because, it sometimes involves being killed. It makes Christians to look at following the Lord Jesus and His Words, "follow me" <u>**in a different light**</u>— **John 12:26:**

> "**If any man serve me, <u>let him follow me</u>**; and where I am, there shall also my servant be: if any man serve me, him will my Father honour."

In ending this chapter, I tell you that as someone now living under the reign of the **antichrist,** you must always remind yourself that **God the Father sent the Lord Jesus Christ into the world to 'lay down His life' for us sinners.** Therefore, His call to, "follow me" should now tell you as a **Tribulation Saint to lay down your life as well.**

You want to obey this call because according to the Lord, "**He who losses his Life for my sake shall find it**" (Matthew 10:39). **Those who will seek to save their lives** *(earthly bodies)* **by accepting the Mark of the Beast will eventually lose their Souls and go to hell.**

My Testimony

I was physically dead for 2 days and the Lord raised me back to life. I know for a fact that this life on earth is not all that there is because **as soon as you die, you immediately find out that life on earth is all about making Jesus your Lord.** Those who did not make Him their Lord quickly realize that they are in great trouble but it is too late; **there is no do-over**. It was while I was dead that I met the Lord Jesus for the first time and **everyone will face Him when they die regardless of their religion**.

Chapter 11
Do Not Kill Yourself for Missing Rapture

Committing Suicide is Not a Godly Answer

I know that many people who professed to be Christians but were left behind after Rapture might be very disappointed and disillusioned. Therefore, many might seek to kill themselves but **killing yourself will put you straight into hell and the Lord cannot help those who kill themselves since their last act on earth is murder!** God did not give anyone permission to kill themselves; actually, **He gets angry with those who destroy man** *(yourself included)* **that He created in His own image.** We are all created in God's image and likeness in Adam. Therefore, I say emphatically that God is not pleased with those who destroy His image *(man or woman).*

'Once Saved Always Saved' Doctrine is a Lie

Do not believe the false doctrines that some denomi-national churches have been telling their members such as those who kill themselves will go to Heaven. Their doctrine that, '<u>once saved always saved' is not true</u>. The doctrine of 'once saved always saved' is a lie from the pit of hell because **killing yourself is a sin. It gets worse if you prayed before doing it** because then, it is a **premeditated and willful sin.** If it is true that, '**once saved always saved,**' why will **the Lord Jesus on Judgment Day** tell some 'Christians' who professed to follow Him, "<u>get away from me, I never knew you</u>;" why will He drive them away from Himself as we read in **Matthew 7:19-23:**

> "Every tree that bringeth not forth good fruit is hewn down, and cast into the fire *(Christians who did not produce godly fruits in their lives).* 20 Wherefore by their fruits ye shall know them. 21 **Not everyone that saith unto me, Lord, Lord, shall enter into the kingdom of heaven;** but he that doeth the will of my Father which is in heaven.
>
> 22 Many will say to me in that day, Lord, Lord, **have we not prophesied in thy name? and in**

> thy name have cast out devils? and in thy name
> done many wonderful works? 23 And then will
> I profess unto them, **I never knew you: depart from
> me, ye that work iniquity** (*doing your own will*)."

The Lord Jesus does not like those who follow Him with lip-service. When He was here on earth, **He called them hypocrites** who say and do not. **This is the precise reason why many professing 'Christians' were left behind after Rapture.** Christianity is not for showmanship; **it is about belonging to the Lord Jesus Christ, following Him** and **living your life according to His Word.**

Suicide is Not the Way to Escape the Antichrist

Many might think that killing themselves is an easy way to get out of being under the reign of the antichrist but it is not God's prescribed way out of your current situation because you will only hasten yourself to eternal damnation and torture. Suicide is a sin and God hates sin as is written in **Ezekiel 18:4:**

> "Behold, **all souls are mine**; as the soul of the father,
> so also the soul of the son is mine: **the soul that
> sinneth, it shall die** (*be eternally separated from God*)."

And in **Matthew 5:21** the Lord said:

> "Ye have heard that it was said by them of old
> time, **thou shalt not kill**; and **whosoever shall
> kill shall be in danger of the judgment**" (*also
> stated in Deuteronomy 5:17*)."

Testimony of a Man Who Killed Himself

I knew a Christian who is an in-law to one of my close friends, this man was diagnosed with an incurable ailment so he promptly killed himself rather than go through the stages of the ailment. According to him, when he faced the Lord, he was shocked because **the Lord was his Judge and not his heavenly Father**; then the Lord said to him, "*I cannot help you because you killed yourself.*" This man learned firsthand that **God hates this sin and that your soul belongs to God. You**

are not allowed or permitted by God to destroy it without facing the consequences which is condemnation to hell.

The Lord in His mercy sent this man back to earth and his body was discovered in time that they were able to revive him. I know that before Rapture occurred, this man was **warning people about the damnable sin of killing oneself.** He preaches that **once you kill yourself, <u>you leave the Lord no room to show you mercy but to judge you as a sinner.</u>**

God's Word is Consistent and Cannot be Broken

As I was writing this section of this book, **the Lord came in and He confirmed what I am telling you about suicide as Truth.** According to the Lord Jesus in **John 10:35,** scripture cannot be broken:

> "...**And the scripture cannot be broken.**"

What the Lord meant by, "**Scripture cannot be broken**" is that the Word of God *(scripture)* is **consistent throughout; <u>it does not contradict itself</u>**. There is no exception for suicide in scripture.

Also, the Word of God says in **Isaiah 55:11**:

> "So shall my word be that goeth forth out of my mouth: **it shall not return unto me void**, but it shall accomplish that which I please, and it shall prosper in the thing whereto I sent it."

Therefore, when you read the **Bible from Genesis to Revelation, there is nowhere in it that God gave permission or made an exception for someone to kill themselves.** Killing yourself is murder pure and simple! It violates God's Word which says, "**Thou shall not kill**" and it makes you a sinner; a killer before God.

You saw that even **King David was disqualified by God from building Him a Temple** because God said, "**David had shed much blood**" even when the wars King David fought were to advance God's nation of Israel. God makes no exception for any sin; even killing in the time of war! Fortunately, for

King David, he lived long enough to repent of all his sins as we see in the book of Psalms; if there was something King David knew, it was how to repent and he did before he died. **You can see that King David's act of repentance is not like <u>those whose last act is the sin of killing themselves</u> that they can never come back to repent of.**

The Following is an excerpt about **Suicide** from **my website:** *maryjministries.org*. Please, read it **in its entirety if you are thinking of killing yourself** as a way out of the situation you are in:

The Truth about Suicide

*"As a result of his sufferings, **Job longed for death**. He wanted God to destroy him so that he could have 'some comfort' from his afflictions **(Job 6:8-11)**. Just like Job, many people **long for death as a way out** of their miseries or the unpleasant situations that they are in. **They think that death is the only way out and that after they die, they will be at rest.** They think that after they have killed themselves, they will then have peace.*

*They think this way because they love themselves so much that they do not want to subject themselves to any further misery. **They do not know that according to the Word of God, they are hastening themselves into a life of eternal damnation, torment and anguish.***

*Assisted suicide or euthanasia is no exception because they are part of killing yourself which is still a sin against God. When you kill yourself or help another person to kill his or herself, **you sin** by violating the Word of God that was spoken by the Lord Jesus in **Matthew 5:21**:*

> *"Ye have heard that it was said by them of old time, **Thou shalt not kill; and whosoever shall kill shall be in danger of the judgment.**"*

*Therefore, when you kill yourself, God has to judge you and send you to hell because suicide is a sin. **Praying before killing yourself is worst because not only is the act of suicide a premeditated act, it becomes a 'willful sin' when you pray before doing it; you are telling God that***

His Word that says not to kill is not important to you.
This is why the Lord Jesus said in **Luke 12:47-48:**

> *"And* **that servant,** *which knew his lord's will, and*
> *prepared not himself, neither did according to his will,*
> **shall be beaten with many stripes.** *But he that knew*
> *not, and did commit things worthy of stripes (killing*
> *yourself),* **shall be beaten with few stripes** *in hell*
> *where there is no coming back from."*

Be it known to you that <u>**those who make it to Heaven are**</u>
<u>**not beaten,**</u> **only those who go to hell are beaten.** *The soul of*
every man and woman lives forever in **Heaven** *or in* **hell.**

Scripture References
The following scriptures refer to those who **abuse,** **destroy,**
maim or kill *their bodies:*

> **"For we must all appear before the judgment seat**
> **of Christ; that every one may receive** <u>**the things**</u>
> <u>**done in his body,**</u> **according to that he hath done,**
> **whether it be good or bad"** *(2 Corinthians 5:10).*

And in **Isaiah 57:21:**

> **"If any man defile the temple of God,** *(the body),*
> **him shall God destroy** *(in hell)."*

When you kill yourself, you not only defile the Temple of God
but you destroy it. Therefore, God counts you among the
wicked because of your final wicked action and God will judge
all the wicked.

The Following are Certain Biblical Judgments on the Wicked:
No peace to the wicked *(Isaiah 57:21)*
God is angry with the wicked *(Psalm 7:11)*
The wicked shall be turned into hell *(Psalm 9:17)*
The Lord is far from the wicked *(Proverbs 15:29)*
The way of the wicked is an abomination *(highly*
distasteful) **to God** *(Proverbs 15:9)*
The wicked are like troubled sea *(Isaiah 57:20)*

From the above scriptures, we see that when someone
commits an act of wickedness like killing his or herself,
it brings upon them the above judgments that have been
pronounced upon the wicked.

Therefore, they cannot have a life of peace after death. It is written in **Hebrews 9:27 "It is appointed unto man once to die, and after that the judgment,"** *but you are not allowed to bring about your own death so, you must not die by your own hand.*

Hell is a Terrible Place to Go

As you can see from God's Word, suicide is not a ticket to a life of 'eternal peace and rest.' **Rather, it is a one-way ticket to a life of eternal damnation from the presence of God and to everlasting torment in the fire of hell.** *It is a place where the people are eaten by worms that will never die!*

If you are contemplating suicide, you need to know the truth from the Word of God that I have outlined so far. **Do not fall for the lies of the devil that 'suicide is an easy way out of a life of pain and anguish.'** *The truth is that no suffering on earth can compare to the eternal anguish in hell and there is no comfort there.*

This means that there is no way to alleviate the pain and sufferings in hell. **Those who want to end their lives by suicide need to know what awaits them on the other side — hell!"**

Find Ways to Comfort Yourself at this Time

Instead of killing yourself, find ways to encourage and comfort yourself and your loved ones. Unless you have no choice, do not isolate yourself but stay in contact with other Christians you can trust. **Pray fervently for the Lord to protect you, your loved ones** and know that the Lord's Word in **Romans 9:28** below holds true for you right now:

> **"For he will finish the work, and cut it short in righteousness:** because **a short work will the Lord make upon the earth."**

God is no respecter of persons because as you can now testify, **He saved all those who put their trust in Him, called upon His Name and walked faithfully with Him during Rapture. Likewise, He will save all those who call upon His Name during the Great Tribulation.** It will help you to remind yourself that the antichrist's reign is only 7 years: even then, the first 3½ years will be bearable compared to the last 3½ years. Therefore, purpose to endure to the end and ask the Lord to hide you.

Chapter 12
Why the Jews Need to Run to their Messiah Now

The Disappearance of Messianic Jews and Innocent Children

I hope that the Almighty God in the Bible or Torah got your attention with the disappearance of faithful Messianic Jews and innocent children all over the world. You know that only the God of Abraham, Isaac and Jacob can do such a thing; He is the Almighty God! I encourage you to open your heart and reconsider your beliefs *(beliefs you were taught)* now that you missed the Lord Jesus Christ; **Yeshua HaMashiach** *(Messiah)* when He came at Rapture.

By not believing in Him before Rapture occurred, you were left behind so do not miss Him again because there will be no more hope once He comes back 7 years after Rapture to destroy all who rejected Him. **What happened at Rapture is what Almighty God always does before He pours out His wrath on the disobedient.** He did it with Noah and with Lot before judging those who were rebellious against Him. In keeping with His righteous pattern, **God sent His Son Jesus Christ to take the righteous out of harm's way because He does not condemn the righteous with the unrighteous.**

The Purpose of God's Covenant with Abraham

As a Jew, you already know that God began His salvation plan for all mankind with the patriarch Abram whom He renamed Abraham. Using King David's descendants *(Abraham's descendants)*, God sent His Son through a virgin Jewish girl to save all humanity. Basically, God and Abraham exchanged sons; meaning that when God saw that Abraham was willing to give up his son Isaac to Him, God released His only begotten Son *(Yeshua HaMashiach)* to save first, Abraham's descendants and then the Gentile nations.

God then made a covenant with Abraham *(and his seed)* so that God's only begotten Son Jesus Christ who will save the world can come forth through Abraham because of his faithfulness to God — **Genesis 15:9-18:**

> "And he said unto him, **Take me an heifer of three years old, and a she goat of three years old, and a ram of three years old, and a turtledove, and a young pigeon.** *10* And he took unto him all these, **and divided them in the midst, and laid each piece one against another:** but the birds divided he not. *11* And when the fowls came down upon the carcases, Abram drove them away. *12* **And it came to pass, that, when the sun went down, and it was dark,** <u>behold a smoking furnace, and a burning lamp *(God)* that passed between those pieces</u>... *18* <u>**In the same day the LORD made a covenant with Abram**</u>..."

This was a very powerful covenant because as you can see from the above scripture, **God Almighty put Himself under the 'Curse of Death' if He ever violated the covenant when He as <u>a Smoking Furnace and a Burning Lamp</u> passed through the pieces of the dead animals.** In other words, according to the terms of the covenant, <u>**the fate of Abraham, his descendants**</u> and <u>**God Almighty will be as those dead animals if any of them ever violate it!**</u> This is how committed God is to this covenant. As you continue reading, you will see how God came in His Word *(Messiah)* to honor this covenant using the lineage of Judah.

Why God Chose Judah as the Lineage of the Messiah

You know that your God is no respecter of persons and that He chooses those whose walk pleases Him. Abraham had 12 grandsons through Jacob but among them only Judah understood the importance of a ransom. The dictionary defines **ransom as the release of a person in return for payment of a demanded price and also a redemption from sin and its consequences.** We see this when their younger brother Benjamin was being held in Egypt by the governor who turned out to be their brother Joseph. Since Simeon was already being held captive in Egypt, their father Jacob would not let them go back to Egypt the second time with Benjamin.

Most of his sons were silent about taking responsibility if they took Benjamin and something happened to him too. Reuben who was unwilling to sacrifice himself or incur his father's wrath, volunteered his sons to be held responsible if he did not bring back Benjamin. **Judah on the other hand, stepped forward and volunteered himself as the <u>ransom</u> for Benjamin his brother.** <u>He told his father to hold him personally responsible if anything bad happens to Benjamin.</u> **When he got to Egypt, God gave him the opportunity to make good on his promise to his father.**

Therefore, when Joseph decided to keep Benjamin in Egypt with him, **Judah stepped forward and offered himself in place of Benjamin to Joseph.** When God saw this, **He chose Judah and his lineage that He will use to bring His beloved Son into the world as the <u>ransom</u> for the sins of both the Jews and the Gentiles.** The Messiah came first to the Jews and then to the Gentiles as revealed when Yeshua was here on earth.

The Lord Jesus Honored the Abrahamic Covenant

When **Yeshua HaMashiach** *(Jesus the Messiah)* was here, **he honored the Abrahamic Covenant.** It is why He told us in **John 4:21-22** that, **salvation is of the Jews**; meaning that <u>God chose to send His Salvation for all humanity through the Jews</u> because of the Abrahamic Covenant:

"Jesus saith unto her, Woman, believe me, the hour cometh, when ye shall neither in this mountain, nor yet at Jerusalem, worship the Father. 22 Ye worship ye know not what: we know what we worship: **for salvation is of the Jews.**"

He further reiterated the importance of this covenant in His conversation with the **Canaanite woman**; a Gentile **who did not have a right to the covenant** and yet, invoked it in **Matthew 15:22-24:**

"And, behold, **a woman of Canaan came out of the same coasts, and cried unto him,** saying, Have mercy on me, O Lord, **thou Son of David** *(meaning Seed of Abraham)*; my daughter is grievously vexed with a devil. 23 **But he answered her not a word**. And his disciples came and besought him, saying, Send her away; for she crieth after us. 24 **But he answered and said, I am not sent but unto the lost sheep of the house of Israel**."

It was not because the Lord did not like the Gentiles but because of the nature of the covenant that God and Abraham made. **It was a 'Death Covenant;' meaning that whoever** (God, Abraham and his descendants including Christ) **violates the covenant dies!** This was why as you noticed in the scripture above, the Lord Jesus could not help the Canaanite woman when **she invoked the Abrahamic Covenant** by calling Him **"thou Son of David."** Unknown to her, **by referring to the covenant between God and Abraham's descendant David,** she immediately **tied the Lord's hands from helping her**.

In response, the Lord told her why He could not help her (*a Gentile*) because as the Son of David — "**I am not sent but unto the lost sheep of the house of Israel.**" He can only help those under the Abrahamic Covenant with God but the woman being led by divine wisdom, worshipped Him and **invoked just the title of His Lordship**; He is Lord of all human beings! As a result, He was able to help her because He is Lord over all humans. We see this in **Matthew 15:25-28:**

> "**Then came she and worshipped him, saying, Lord, help me.** 26 But he answered and said, It is not meet to take the children's bread, and to cast it to dogs. 27 And she said, Truth, Lord: yet the dogs eat of the crumbs which fall from their masters' table. 28 Then Jesus answered and said unto her, O woman, great is thy faith: be it unto thee even as thou wilt. And her daughter was made whole from that very hour."

As you can see, the Lord was pleased with her faith and her tenacity! He healed her daughter. I talked about this in detail in one of my books titled, *Understanding the Power of Covenants.*

Our God is a God of covenant; **He honors all our covenants even when they are with the devil as Adam did.**

Another Reason Why Christ was Sent to the Jews

By sending His Son Jesus Christ to humanity through the nation of Israel, <u>God fulfilled His promise to Abraham that through him shall all the nations on the earth be blessed</u> as recorded in **Genesis 22:15-18:**

"And the angel of the LORD called unto Abraham out of heaven the second time, *16* And said, By myself have I sworn, saith the LORD, <u>for because thou hast done this thing, and hast not withheld thy son, thine only son</u>: *17* **That in blessing I will bless thee, and in multiplying I will multiply thy seed as the stars of the heaven,** and as the sand which is upon the sea shore; and thy seed shall possess the gate of his enemies; *18* **And in thy seed shall all the nations of the earth be blessed;** because thou hast obeyed my voice."

Also, in **Genesis 18:17-18:**

"And the LORD said, Shall I hide from Abraham that thing which I do; *18* **Seeing that Abraham shall surely become a great and mighty nation, and <u>all the nations of the earth shall be blessed in him</u>?**"

The Apostle Paul wrote about the fact that <u>God first sent His salvation to the Jews because of the covenant He made with Abraham</u> as we see in **Galatians 4:4-5:**

"**But when the fulness of the time was come, <u>God sent forth his Son, made of a woman, made under the law</u>,** *5* <u>**To redeem them that were under the law**</u>, that we might receive the adoption of sons."

Today, all the nations look to the Lord Jesus to recieve God's Abrahamic blessings. All human blessings now come through the Lord Jesus; the Seed of Abraham.

Jesus as God's Promised Prophet to the Jews

As a Jew, you know that **God told Moses about raising up a Prophet to the Jewish people** that will be like Moses and whom they should hear in all things. According to God, whoever does not hear this Prophet will be destroyed — **Deuteronomy 18:15-19:**

> "**The LORD thy God will raise up unto thee a Prophet from the midst of thee, of thy brethren, like unto me; unto him ye shall hearken;** 16 According to all that thou desiredst of the LORD thy God in Horeb in the day of the assembly, saying, Let me not hear again the voice of the LORD my God, neither let me see this great fire any more, that I die not. 17 And the LORD said unto me, They have well spoken that which they have spoken.
>
> 18 **I will raise them up a Prophet from among their brethren, like unto thee, and will put my words in his mouth; and he shall speak unto them all that I shall command him.** 19 And it shall come to pass, that **whosoever will not hearken unto my words which he shall speak in my name, I will require it of him.**"

And also in **Isaiah 7:14:**

> "Therefore the Lord himself shall give you a sign; Behold, a virgin shall conceive, and bear a son, and shall call his name **Immanuel** (*God with us*)."

It is repeated in **Isaiah 9:6:**

> "For unto us a child is born, unto us a son is given: and the government shall be upon his shoulder: and his name shall be called **Wonderful, Counsellor, The Mighty God, The Everlasting Father, The Prince of Peace.**"

When the Lord Jesus was here, He told the Jews that God the Father sent Him and gave Him the words to speak. He also told them that if they do not believe in Him, they will die in their sins in **John 12:44-50:**

"Jesus cried and said, **He that believeth on me, believeth not on me, but on him that sent me.** 45 **And he that seeth me seeth him that sent me.** 46 I am come a light into the world, that whosoever believeth on me should not abide in darkness. 47 And if any man hear my words, and believe not, I judge him not: for I came not to judge the world, but to save the world.

48 **He that rejecteth me, and receiveth not my words, hath one that judgeth him: the word that I have spoken, the same shall judge him in the last day.** 49 <u>**For I have not spoken of myself; but the Father which sent me, he gave me a commandment, what I should say, and what I should speak**</u>. 50 And I know that his commandment is life everlasting: <u>**whatsoever I speak therefore, even as the Father said unto me, so I speak**</u>."

And in **John 8:24:**

"I said therefore unto you, **that ye shall die in your sins**: for <u>**if ye believe not that I am he**</u> *(that Prophet)*, <u>**ye shall die in your sins**</u>."

The Lord Jesus as the Scapegoat

God required the Jewish High Priest to select two goats annually for sin offerings. One of the goats was to carry the sins of all the people and be driven into the wilderness after the High Priest had laid his hands on its head and confessed the sins of the people upon it. **The Lord Jesus fulfilled this role once and for all for the Jews and the Gentiles when He was led outside the city walls bearing our sin and crucified on the Cross**.

It is God's reason why there has been no animal sacrifices in Israel for over 2,000 years because Christ forever fulfilled the role of the Scapegoat for us all. Therefore, no more animal sacrifices are needed; it was fully accomplished by Christ and God is pleased. **Do not fall for the attempts by religious zealots to bring back the animal sacrifices** during the reign of the antichrist. God has said that the blood of bulls and goats are not good enough for Him as we see in **Hebrews 10:4-10**:

> **"For it is not possible that the blood of bulls and of goats should take away sins.** 5 Wherefore when he *(Yeshua)* cometh into the world, he saith, **Sacrifice and offering thou wouldest not**, but <u>a body hast thou prepared me</u>: 6 **In burnt offerings and sacrifices for sin thou hast had no pleasure.** 7 Then said I, Lo, I come (in the volume of the book it is written of me,) to do thy will, O God.
>
> 8 Above when he said, Sacrifice and offering and burnt offerings and offering for sin thou wouldest not, neither hadst pleasure therein; **which are <u>offered by the law</u>**; 9 Then said he, Lo, I come to do thy will, O God. **He taketh away the first** *(the law; Old Testament)*, **that he may establish the second** *(New Testament).* 10 <u>**By the which will we are sanctified through the offering of the body of Jesus Christ once for all**</u>."

The Jews' Rejection of Christ Brought Salvation to the Gentiles

When the Jews rejected Christ, **they violated the Abrahamic Covenant** and as result, God extended salvation to the Gentiles because before then as Jesus said, salvation is of the Jews. We see the Jewish rejection of Christ recorded in **John 1:1-12:**

> **"In the beginning was the <u>Word,</u> and the Word was <u>with God,</u> and the Word <u>was God</u>. 2 The same was in the beginning with God. 3 All things were made by him; and without him was not any thing made that was made. 4 <u>In him was life; and the life was the light of men</u>.** 5 And the light shineth in darkness; and the darkness comprehended it not. 6

There was a man sent from God, whose name was John. 7 The same came for a witness, to bear witness of the Light, that all men through him might believe.

8 He was not that Light, but was sent to bear witness of that Light. 9 **That was the true Light, which lighteth every man that cometh into the world.** He *(Christ)* was in the world, and the world was made by him, and the world knew him not. 11 **He came unto his own** *(the Jews)*, **and his own received him not.** 12 **But as many as received him, to them** *(Jews and Gentiles)* **gave he power to become the sons of God,** even to them that believe on his name."

As you have just read, it was only after the Jews rejected Jesus Christ that salvation was made available to the **Gentile nations** *(non-Jewish nations)* but **it does not mean that God has forever cast off the Jews.** Rather, **their rejection of Christ gave the pagan Gentile nations who had not previously chosen to serve the Almighty God, the opportunity to also receive God's salvation.** Meaning that when the Lord Jesus was rejected by the Jews and as they sought to kill Him, **He went to Capernaum** *(a Gentile city)* **and dwelt there.** Prior to this, **the Gentile nations were sitting in darkness** *(had no light from God)* as recorded in **Matthew 4:13-17:**

"**And leaving Nazareth, he** *(Jesus)* **came and dwelt in Capernaum,** which is upon the sea coast, in the borders of Zebulon and Naphtali: 14 That it might be fulfilled which was spoken by Esaias the prophet, saying, 15 **The land of Zebulon, and the land of Nephthalim, by the way of the sea, beyond Jordan, Galilee of the Gentiles;** 16 **The people which sat in darkness saw great light; and to them which sat in the region and shadow of death light is sprung up.** 17 From that time Jesus began to preach, and to say, Repent: for the kingdom of heaven is at hand."

Christians Should not be Antisemitic or Haters of Jews

Know that the <u>Gentile nations were grafted into Israel's True Olive Tree</u>; the Lord Jesus Christ so, do not think that God is done with Israel or be puffed up against the Jews. God will graft them back into their Natural Vine; Christ the Jew! We see this recorded in **Romans 11:22-24:**

> "<u>Behold therefore the goodness and severity of God</u>: on them which fell *(Jews)*, severity; but toward thee, goodness, if thou continue in his goodness: otherwise thou also shalt be cut off. 23 And they *(Jews)* also, **if they abide not still in unbelief, shall be graffed in**: for God is able to graff them in again.
>
> <u>24 For if thou wert cut out of the olive tree which is wild by nature,</u> and **wert graffed contrary to nature** into a good olive tree: **how much more shall these, which be the natural branches, be graffed into their own olive tree?**"

You cannot love the Lord Jesus and hate the Jews because He is a Jew. A true Christian will love the Jews and thank God that He gave us a Savior through them. We are to always remember that God's Word to Abraham also applies to all his descendants — **Genesis 12:1-3:**

> "Now the LORD had said unto Abram, Get thee out of thy country, and from thy kindred, and from thy father's house, unto a land that I will shew thee: 2 <u>And I will make of thee a great nation,</u> and **I will bless thee, and make thy name great; and thou shalt be a blessing:** 3 **<u>And I will bless them that bless thee, and curse him that curseth thee</u>**: and in thee shall all families of the earth be blessed."

The Lord's Second Coming is to Save the Jews

God will turn His attention to the Jews once the time that

He allotted the Gentiles is fulfilled; **the end of the reign of the antichrist**. Make no mistake about it; He is their Messiah and He loves them. He died for them and the rest of the world; they are God's covenant children with Abraham. As always, He will arise and save them when they are endangered by the antichrist who will **seek to annihilate them.** At first, the antichrist will make a **Peace Covenant** with Israel but he will break the terms of the covenant after 3½ years as recorded in **Daniel 9:27:**

> "And he shall confirm the covenant with many for one week *(7 years):* **and in the midst of the week he shall cause the sacrifice and the oblation to cease**, and for the overspreading of abominations <u>he shall make it desolate</u>, even until the consummation, and that determined shall be poured upon the desolate."

The Lord Jesus confirmed that the antichrist will rise against the Jews and try to destroy them in **Mark 13:14-15:**

> "**But when ye** *(Jews)* **shall see** <u>the abomination of desolation</u>**, spoken of by Daniel the prophet, standing where it ought not**, (let him that readeth understand,) **then let them that be in Judaea flee to the mountains.** 15 And let him that is on the housetop not go down into the house, neither enter therein, to take anything out of his house."

Before this turn of events, **the antichrist will <u>help the Jews to build a Temple in Jerusalem</u> but he shall come into the Temple, sit in it and declare himself to be God.** The Jews will promptly reject him and this will arouse his anger against them and he will gather the nations together to war against the Jews to destroy them all. <u>**Just as Israel sees no hope of overcoming him, the Messiah will appear in the sky to destroy him and all the nations that surrounded Jerusalem**</u> as recorded in **2 Thessalonians 2:3-10:**

"Let no man deceive you by any means: for that day shall not come, except there come a falling away first, and that man of sin be revealed, the son of perdition; 4 **Who opposeth and exalteth himself above all that is called God**, or that is worshipped; **so that he as God sitteth in the temple of God, shewing himself that he is God**...

8 And then shall **that Wicked** (*antichrist*) **be revealed, whom the Lord shall consume with the spirit of his mouth, and shall destroy with the brightness of his coming:** 9 Even him, **whose coming is after the working of Satan with all power and signs and lying wonders,** 10 And with all deceivableness of unrighteousness in them that perish; because they received not the love of the truth, that they might be saved."

And **Zachariah 14:2-5** also revealed that the Lord Himself will come to save Israel from the antichrist and his forces:

"For I will gather all nations against Jerusalem to battle; and the city shall be taken, and the houses rifled, and the women ravished; and half of the city shall go forth into captivity, and the residue of the people shall not be cut off from the city. 3 **Then shall the Lord go forth, and fight against those nations, as when he fought in the day of battle.**

4 **And his feet shall stand in that day upon the mount of Olives, which is before Jerusalem on the east,** and the mount of Olives shall cleave in the midst thereof toward the east and toward the west, and there shall be a very great valley; and half of the mountain shall remove toward the north, and half of it toward the south. 5 And ye shall flee to the valley of the mountains; for the valley of the mountains shall reach unto Azal: yea, ye shall flee, like as ye fled from before the

earthquake in the days of Uzziah king of Judah: and **the Lord my God shall come, and all the saints with thee.**"

Christ's Millennial Reign will be in Jerusalem

As a Christian, do not boast yourself against the Jews or the nation of Israel because **Christ's Millennial Reign will be in Jerusalem and all the redeemed souls of both Jews and Gentiles with Him.** This means that you will live, reign and rule with Him from Jerusalem so **how can you speak against your eternal home and your eternal brethren?** The Apostle Paul tells us in **Galatians 3:27-29** that both Jew and Gentile believers in Christ are all **One New Man**:

"For as many of you as have been baptized into Christ have put on Christ. *28* **There is neither Jew nor Greek, there is neither bond nor free, there is neither male nor female: for ye are all one in Christ Jesus**. *29* And if ye be Christ's, then are ye Abraham's seed, and heirs according to the promise."

Also, in **Ephesians 2:15** we learn that:

"*(Messiah)*Having abolished in his flesh the enmity, even the law of commandments contained in ordinances; for **to make in himself of twain <u>one new man</u>** *(Jews and Gentiles),* **so making peace.**"

We are commanded to pray for the peace of Jerusalem as we see in **Psalm 122:6:**

"**Pray for the peace of Jerusalem: <u>they shall prosper that love thee</u>.**"

There is actually a blessing of prosperity for praying for the peace of Jerusalem. God will always bless you when you pray for the peace of Jerusalem and Israel. Remember that Jacob whom God surnamed Israel is Abraham's descendant so, in blessing him, you too receive a blessing from God.

What All Jews Need to Do Now

As a Jew, you are very aware of all the atrocities that have been committed against the Jews by <u>those who used the name of Jesus Christ to foster their evil desires</u>. They committed all their evil atrocities against the Jews because they did not know Christ, His ways and His teachings. They were not Christ's followers because <u>Christ came to save the Jews first before the Gentiles as you have read</u>. **It is now time for you to stop relying on other people's account of who the Lord Jesus Christ is and find out for yourself who He really is; the Jewish Messiah and Savior of the world.**

It is time for you to receive the Lord Jesus as your Messiah because if you wait any longer after Rapture has occurred, **you may not able to spiritually fight the forces of the antichrist that will deceive people to take his Mark**. He will use **mind control** on all who are not under the Messiah's covering. You need to turn to your Messiah; the Lord Jesus Christ so that He can keep you at this perilous time. He is waiting for you with open arms so run to Him.

No Jew Should Receive the Mark of the Antichrist

FYI: When **Yeshua HaMashiach** appears at His Second Coming to save the Jews, **only the Jews who have not received the Mark or the name of the Beast or antichrist can be saved.** All those who received the Mark or the number of his name *(666)* will be cast into the Lake of Fire because **the Mark means they chose the devil over God**. Know that once a person chooses the Mark, **the decision cannot be reversed**; the person is doomed forever.

The Steps and Message of Salvation

To **receive the Lord Jesus as your Savior**, first, you must believe the **Good News** of the **Word of God** in **John 3:16-18:**

> **"For God so loved the world, that he gave his only begotten Son, that whosoever believeth in him should not perish, but have everlasting life.** For God sent not his Son into the world to

condemn the world; but that the world through him might be saved. *18* **He that believeth on him is not condemned: but <u>he that believeth not is condemned already</u>,** because he hath not believed in the name of the only begotten Son of God."

You must also believe that the Lord Jesus is **that Prophet which God promised the Jews through Moses** and that **He is the only way that you can get to God in Heaven** as stated in **Romans 10:9-10:**

"That if thou shalt **confess with thy mouth the Lord Jesus,** and **shalt believe in thine heart that God hath raised him from the dead, thou shalt be saved.** *10* For **with the heart man believeth unto righteousness;** and with **the mouth confession is made unto salvation."**

Pray this Prayer below **aloud** if you **believe** what is written in the Scriptures above:

The Prayer of Salvation

"Father, in the name of the Lord Jesus, I come to You. I am sorry for not believing all these years that Jesus Christ is Your Son and that He is my Messiah and my God. Today, I forgive all the people that had taught me to reject and hate Your Son Jesus Christ for I now know that they were wrong.

<u>I believe that Jesus Christ is Your Son and my Messiah who came into the world in the flesh and was crucified on the Cross for my sins. I believe that He died on the Cross from all my sins and was buried but on the third day, You raised Him from the dead</u>.

Today, I confess with my mouth and I believe it in my heart that Jesus Christ is my Lord. Lord Jesus, **<u>I repent of my all sins, I ask You to forgive me and wash me with Your blood from all my sins</u>.** Please, **come into my heart and be my Lord** for I surrender to Your

Lordship this day and forever. Give me Your eternal life for I declare that I belong to You from now on.

Also, **I ask You to give me Your Holy Spirit** to keep me in Your will, teach me the Bible, lead and protect me. I choose to do only those things that please You from now on. Father, I believe that You heard me and that I am now your child. Thank You for giving me Your Son and Your Holy Spirit; I receive them in the name of the Lord Jesus; Amen."

Once you receive the Lord Jesus as your Messiah, you will dance and sing with the greatest joy you will ever know.

Note: Get the New King James Bible and learn about your Messiah and your new life in Him.

Chapter 13
To Muslims Who Say that, 'God Cannot Have a Son'

If you were **practicing Islam** before Rapture *(the taking away of Christians and all the babies in the world)* occurred, and you **believed that God cannot have a Son**, you are now living in a world after **God's Son** *(Jesus Christ)* whom you did not believe in, came and **took out of the world, all those who believed in Him including your babies!**

The disappearance of your babies along with Christians who walked faithfully with the Lord Jesus Christ should prove to you that there is only One God and that He indeed, has a Son called Jesus Christ. It should also prove to you that the God of the Bible is real **and you should be worshiping Him.** I mean no disrespect, **Allah did not keep your babies from being taken by the Almighty God of the Bible.**

The following information is from *Chapter 1* of this book. It tells you why **the only Living and True God of the Bible took your babies. You need an open mind concerning the God of the Bible** and to read this book to the end. **I do sincerely believe that the information below will help you if you are genuinely seeking answers about the occurrence of Rapture.**

Excerpt from *Chapter 1* of this book:

"Why Will God Take the Children?
Remember that when He was here physically, the **Lord Jesus was preaching to everyday people with little children. Children are born innocent just as Adam and Eve were, until they get corrupted by sin.** *While child-ren are* **still innocent, God protects and keeps** *them but when they* **learn to hide their wrong doings, they lose their innocence.**

Every child reaches this **age of covering up wrong doing** *at* **different times.** *A good example is the* **cookie jar.** *When a child is* **young and innocent** *and the mother tells the child to stay away from the cookie jar, the child might go and take* *a cookie and eat it. When the mother comes and sees cookie crumbs on the face of the child and she asks the child if he took a cookie from the jar,* **the child smiles and says no without realizing that the evidence of his actions are all over his face.**

As this same child gets older and **learns that disobedience has consequences,** *when the mother tells the child to stay out of the cookie jar, and he disobeys,* **takes a cookie but carefully rearranges the cookies in the jar to cover up his action so that the mother will not know that one cookie is missing. Also, the child carefully wipes his face so that there is no evidence of what he did.** *This age at which the* **child knows to cover up his actions and lie about it is** *called the* **'Age of Accountability.'**

The action of the child proves that the child does not want to be held accountable for his disobedience by covering it up. This action (sin), means that **the child now knows the difference between right and wrong.** *People get to this stage of lying at different ages and God sees it all from Heaven; He knows when the child stops being innocent.*

Unfortunately, when this happens, **sin** *(wrong doing)* **separates** *them from* **God's Presence. Therefore, at Rapture, the Lord only took all the children that have not yet learned how to cover up their wrong doing;** *they do not know sin. Also, they have not rejected the Lord Jesus Christ as their older siblings and parents have.*

What the Lord Jesus Said about the Little Children

The Lord Jesus cares about the little children and this is what He said concerning them in **Matthew 18:10:**

> **"Take heed that ye despise not one of these little ones; for I say unto you, That in heaven their angels** (spirits) **do always behold the face of my Father which is in heaven."**

And in **Matthew 19:13-14:**

> *"Then were there brought unto him little children, that he should put his hands on them, and pray: and the disciples rebuked them. 14 But Jesus said,* **Suffer little children,**

and forbid them not, to come unto me: for of such is the kingdom of heaven. 15 And he laid his hands on them, and departed thence."

In **Mark 10:15**, He said:

*"Verily I say unto you, **Whosoever shall not receive the kingdom of God as a little child**, he shall not enter therein."*

He also said in **Matthew 18:14:**

"Even so it is not the will of your Father which is in heaven, that one of these little ones should perish."

You see, God did not want the little children to perish. He took them and did not leave them behind."

The Bible is the Accurate Word of God

Just to tell you how accurate the Word of God in the Bible is, I wrote this book before Rapture occurred and millions of people who are now in Heaven are watching you as you read it. This book tells you what the Bible says will happen and it did!

Before Rapture, many Christians tried to tell a lot of Muslims about the Good News of the Gospel of the Lord Jesus Christ; that He came into the world as God's Son to save all humanity from sin by dying on the Cross.

Unfortunately, apart from viewing the Lord Jesus as a 'Good Prophet,' for a lot of them, their **stumbling block was that Jesus is called the <u>Son of God</u>.** They out rightly refused to even consider that Almighty God; the Creator of Heaven and Earth who can do anything, can provide Himself with a Son. Think about it, if God can give human beings children, why can He not provide Himself with a Son when He needs one?

<u>Maybe now that Rapture has occurred and your babies or the babies of your fellow Muslims have also disappeared</u> along with the faithful Christians, God can finally get your attention. Do not make the **same mistake of not believing in**

the Lord Jesus Christ; the Son of God after Rapture occurred. If you continue in **unbelief, you will have no choice but to receive the Mark of the Beast** *(the Mark or name of the 'New World Leader')* **because of the** <u>mind control</u> **used by him. Anyone who gets the Mark will be condemned to hell with him.**

How God Can Have a Son

The definition of a son is **one's male descendant.** Remember that this chapter is for those who think that it is **impossible,** <u>**blasphemous**</u> or <u>**abominable**</u> to say that the **Almighty God has a Son.** Many Muslims have this belief because **Islam decries the very notion of entertaining the belief that God has a Son** <u>but now you will see below that this Islamic belief is very wrong!</u>

The reason for this **erroneous Islamic belief** is that in the **mind of many Muslims,** for God to have a Son, **He would have to be involved in a carnal act which is incomprehensible!** Not only Muslims, but everyone should consider it an **insult to think that the Most Righteous God would** <u>be involved in a carnal act; the</u> <u>**Almighty God is Holy and can never be involved in a carnal act.**</u> As the Creator of the universe and all human souls, **God does not need a physical relationship with a woman to produce a Son as you will see below.**

How God Created His First Son; Adam

Many people do not realize that all humanity descended from God's first son; **Adam;** meaning **Man!** For your information, **when God created His first son Adam;** from whom we all descended, <u>**no carnal act was involved**</u>. This is written in **Genesis 2:7-23:**

> "**And the LORD God formed man** *(Adam)* **of the** <u>**dust of the ground,**</u> **and breathed into his nostrils the** <u>**Breath of Life**</u> *(His Spirit);* **and man became a Living Soul** *(meaning came alive)... 15* **And the LORD God took the Man,** and put him into the **Garden of Eden** *(Earth)* **to dress it and to keep it**...

And **the LORD God caused a deep sleep to fall upon Adam, and he slept**: and he *(God)* **took one of his ribs, and closed up the flesh instead thereof;** 22 And **the rib, which the LORD God had taken from man, made he a woman**, and **brought her unto the man.** 23 And **Adam said, This is now bone of my bones, and flesh of my flesh: she shall be called Woman, because she was taken out of Man."**

God called this being that **He created out of clay or dust Adam**; meaning **Man** *(His first son).* **God gave humanity the name Adam;** then, Adam called his own rib *(his wife)* **Woman. God created humanity as Male and Female but modern man sought to change God's order of creation and it resulted in the dysfunctional world that you now find yourself.**

From the above scriptures, **you can see that a carnal act was not involved in God's Creation of Adam** and that the **'Breath of God'** was the **spirit in Adam** and **in all humanity to this day!** If you do not believe this, you will note that the day that **'God's Breath' departs** from **any human being**, that **person dies** because **without God's breath** *(Spirit)*, **none of us would have life.** You can see that **all God needed to Create His first son; Adam** was a **'Lump of Clay'** and **not a carnal act.**

Again, to create Adam, **Elohim simply breathed His breath into a 'Lump of Clay' and it came alive as the first son of God** because of **God's breath** in him! This is why **Adam** is a part of God called the **son of God;** His breath in Adam unites them as one. We see this in **Luke 3:23-38** in the genealogy of Joseph; Mary's husband which was traced all the way back to the first man — Adam:

"And Jesus himself began to be about thirty years of age, being *(as was supposed)* the son of Joseph, which was the son of **Heli**, 24 Which was the son of **Matthat**, which was the son of **Levi**, which was the son of **Melchi**...38 Which was the son of **Enos**, which was the son of **Seth,** *(Cain's bother)* which was the son of **Adam,** which was **the Son of God.**"

Note that not just Joseph and Mary's genealogies, but **all humanity's genealogy goes all the way back to Adam; the first son of God!** This is why **man is the most unique** of all of God's Creation.

God's Desire for a Son, His Judgment and His Mercy in the Garden

The Bible tells us in **Genesis 1:26** that the **creation** of Adam began with a desire that God had about having a **son that would exercise dominion or rule the earth for Him.** This is where the term, 'Landlord' came from; **God made Adam the Lord of the earth** to rule over everything on earth:

> "And God said, **Let us make man** (Adam) **in our image, after our likeness** *(a son in His image and likeness)*: and **let them have dominion** *(rule)* **over the fish of the sea, and over the fowl of the air, and over the cattle, and over all the earth,** and **over every creeping thing** that creepeth upon the earth."

Unfortunately, as we already saw, **Adam willfully sinned by rebelling against God's commandment to him and plunged all humanity into sin with him.** This is because all humanity came from Adam's Seed *(from his loins)* and Eve is the mother of all living souls. All these happened spiritually before God dispatched us to earth from the loins of Adam. **We all existed spiritually with God in Adam before sin separated us from God. This is why God brings every human being to the earth so that we can reconnect with Him and receive God's Eternal Life.** This is the **main purpose** why all human beings are here on earth — to be reconnected with God by His Son!

As a result of Adam and Eve's sin which was passed down to us, **we lost the ability to rule over everything on the Planet Earth as God had originally intended for us to do.** But **God in His mercy, sacrificed a LAMB** *(His Son Jesus Christ)* and used **His blood and skin to cover Adam and his wife's sin** in the Garden of Eden before driving them out — **Genesis 3:17-24:**

> **"And unto Adam he said, <u>Because thou hast hearkened unto the voice of thy wife, and hast eaten of the tree, of which I commanded thee, saying, Thou shalt not eat of it: cursed is the ground for thy sake;</u>** in sorrow shalt thou eat of it all the days of thy life; 18 Thorns also and thistles shall it bring forth to *thee (meant to irritate Adam as he farms)*; and thou shalt eat the herb of the field;
>
> 19 In the sweat of thy face shalt thou eat bread, **till thou return unto the ground; for out of it wast thou taken: for dust thou art, and unto dust shalt thou return.** 20 And Adam called his wife's name Eve; because she was the mother of all living. 21 **Unto Adam also and to his wife did the LORD God make coats of skins, and clothed them.**
>
> 22 And the LORD God said, Behold, the man is become as one of us, to know good and evil: and now, lest he put forth his hand, and take also of the tree of life, and eat, and live forever: 23 **<u>Therefore the LORD God sent him forth</u> from the garden of Eden**, **to till the ground from whence he was taken** *(meaning made)*. 24 **So he drove out the man**; and he placed at the east of the garden of Eden Cherubims, and a flaming sword which turned every way, **to keep the way of the tree of life** *(He drove him away so that he does eat the fruit from the Tree of Life and live forever in miseries)."*

For all those who want to know why the world is so full of evil, this is how all human beings **became separated from God by sin. This rebellion** *(disobedience)* **by Adam; the first man is the beginning of all the sins in the world today**. Had God not blocked their way in the Garden of Eden, they would have eaten the fruit from the Tree of Life. This means that humanity would have been living in misery, in sicknesses and diseases for all of eternity with no way out.

The saddest thing about the evil *(the fruit of sin)* in the world is that as we saw in a previous chapter, **Eve desired to have a taste of evil against God's commandment and Adam joined her and tasted evil for all mankind;** they chose to experience evil!

God Had to Provide Himself a Righteous Son to Solve the Problem of Sin

As stated before, all of humanity became **enslaved by the devil with sin** since Adam's disobedience but God spiritually took care of the problem of sin in the Garden of Eden when it occurred. **He sacrificed a Lamb;** His Son Jesus Christ! This <u>truth</u> is repeated in all the chapters of this book because this **'spiritual sacrifice' by God was manifested in the physical sacrifice of His Son Jesus on the Cross** in Jerusalem for the sins of all of Adam's descendants. This was the reason that **God sent the Lord Jesus to earth to be born in an animal stable in order to be sacrificed as a Lamb.** In other words, God needed a son to accomplish our salvation and deliver us from the devil.

Why the Islamic Ramadan Ram or Lamb Cannot Take Away Sin

Every year, Muslims engage in the Ramadan fast and at the end, sacrifice a ram or a lamb in hope of appeasing God about their sins. They learned this tradition from Abraham's son called Ishmael. This 'Abrahamic Tradition' which goes all the way back to Adam was to remind people and **prepare the way for the future physical manifestation of the 'sacrifice of God's Son'** on earth.

When God was ready to bring forth His Son, God looked for a man who would obey His commandment and He chose Abraham. First, **He tested Abraham to see if he would sacrifice his son Isaac to Him.** When Abraham obeyed, God kept him from killing Isaac and released a Lamb to him instead. <u>**The Lamb symbolized the Lord Jesus Christ;**</u> **God's own Son whom He had already sacrificed spiritually in the Garden of Eden** on the day that Adam and Eve sinned. **Abraham's** willingness to give up his son Isaac to God moved God to also give up His own Son; Jesus Christ for humanity!

God had to sacrifice His own Son because the blood of bulls, rams, lambs and goats **cannot take away human sin; only God's own blood can. This is why God needed a Son that He can sacrifice or punish for the sins of the world** as we see in **Hebrews 10:3-7:**

> "But in those sacrifices there is a remembrance again made of sins every year. 4 **For it is not possible that the blood of bulls and of goats should take away sins.** 5 Wherefore when he *(Jesus Christ)* cometh into the world, he saith, **Sacrifice and offering** thou wouldest not *(you do not like)*, but a body *(a human body)* **hast thou prepared me**: 6 **In burnt offerings and sacrifices for sin thou hast had no pleasure.** 7 Then said I, Lo, I come *(in the volume of the book [Bible] it is written of me)* to do thy will, O God *(go to the Cross for our sins)*."

God's ways are mysterious and you cannot lean to your own understanding concerning them. **This is why you should not believe that God is unable to provide Himself a Son when the future of all humanity depends on what He would do on the Cross with His Son for our sins!**

How the Lord Jesus was Conceived in the Womb

I want you to know that **500 years** before the Lord Jesus was born, **God promised the Jewish people a Savior in Isaiah 9:6:**

> "For unto us a child is born, unto us a son is given: and the government shall be upon his shoulder: and his name shall be called **Wonderful, Counsellor, The mighty God, The everlasting Father, The Prince of Peace**."

And also, in **Isaiah 7:14-15** which states that a virgin shall conceive and give birth to a son:

"...**Behold, <u>a virgin shall conceive, and bear a son</u>, and shall call his name Immanuel** *(meaning God with us)*. 15 Butter and honey shall he eat, **that he may know to <u>refuse the evil, and</u> <u>choose the good</u>** *(this is something God's first son Adam failed to do)."*

As a result of the prophecy about **a virgin conceiving a child and before** the **coming of the Lord Jesus into the world,** every Jewish girl hoped to be **the mother of the Messiah; Savior.** When the time finally came for **God to manifest on earth the 'sacrifice of His Son;' the Lamb, <u>He sent His Word</u> into the womb of a virgin teenage girl called Mary**.

In other words, **God by His Holy Spirit, sent <u>His spoken Word</u>** through the Angel Gabriel to a virgin named Mary. What happened was that, when the Angel Gabriel spoke God's Word to Mary, **the Word of God activated and fertilized one of Mary's ovaries to become a baby in her womb — Luke 1:28-32:**

"**And the angel came in unto her, and said, Hail, thou that art highly favoured, the Lord is with thee: blessed art thou among women.** 29 And when she saw him, she was troubled at his saying, and cast in her mind what manner of salutation this should be. 30 And the angel said unto her, Fear not, Mary: for thou hast found favour with God. 31 **And, behold, <u>thou shalt conceive in thy womb, and bring forth a son, and shalt call his name JESUS.</u>**

32 **He shall be great, and shall be called the Son of the Highest: and the Lord God shall give unto him the throne of his father David** *(this is the Word of God Gabriel was sent to speak to Mary).* 34 Then said Mary unto the angel, **How shall this be, seeing I know not a man?** 35 And the angel answered and said unto her, **The Holy Ghost shall come upon thee, and the power of the Highest shall overshadow thee: therefore also that holy thing which shall be born of thee shall be called the Son of God."**

<u>This is the same Word of God that He spoke to create the Heaven and earth</u>. **Note that God did not have to engage in a carnal act to produce the Lord Jesus as His Son**. He just spoke His Word through an angel and it became a baby; He did not use dust or clay as He did with the first Adam. For God to '**beget**' or '**reproduce Himself**' in the Lord Jesus Christ, He used something better than clay — His own Word which <u>makes the Lord Jesus Christ part of Him.</u>

Meaning that, God just simply sent the Lord Jesus forth from His mouth! We all know that a person and his or her word are one; you cannot separate a person from the word out of their mouth. Neither can you do the same with God Almighty and His Word Jesus Christ; they are one. This is why the Apostle John wrote the following about who the Lord Jesus is in **John 1:1-4**:

> "**In the beginning was <u>the Word</u>** (Jesus)**, and <u>the Word was with God</u>, and <u>the Word was God</u>.** 2 The same was in the beginning with God. 3 **All things were made by him**; and **without him was not anything made that was made** (*God creates by speaking His Word; Jesus*). 4 In him was life; and the life was the light of men."

A fact you should know is that a baby in the womb has a separate blood circulatory system from its mother; **the Lord Jesus has God's blood. This is why you must know the Lord Jesus as the Word of God for yourself and receive His life which is the Life of God Almighty.**

God Almighty Confirmed that Jesus is His Son

God the Father bore witness to the truth that Jesus is His Son — **Luke 3:21-22:**

> "Now when all the people were baptized, **it came to pass, that Jesus also being baptized, and praying, the heaven was opened,** 22 **And the Holy Ghost descended in a bodily shape like a**

dove upon him, and a voice came from heaven *(God)*, which said, **Thou art my beloved Son; in thee I am well pleased.**"

On the Day of Jesus's Transfiguration

This is the day that the Lord Jesus showed His disciples that **He is God by briefly stepping into His God-state** before their eyes as recorded in **Matthew 17:2-5:**

> "And *(Jesus)* **was transfigured before them: and his face did shine as the sun, and his raiment was white as the light.** *3* And, behold, there appeared unto them Moses and Elias talking with him. Behold, a bright cloud overshadowed them: and behold **a voice out of the cloud** *(God the Father's voice)*, **which said, This is my beloved Son, in whom I am well pleased; hear ye him.**"

God's message to every human being is; **hear my Son and obey His every Word** because they are the **Words of the Almighty God.**

The Lord Jesus Stated that He is the Son of God

Some people **claim that the Lord Jesus never said that He was the Son of God** but what they do not know is that when the Lord was asked about His identity, **He Himself confirmed that He is the Son of God** in **John 10:36-38.** You can read His Own Words for yourself:

> "Say ye of him, whom the Father hath sanctified, and sent into the world, Thou blasphemest; because **I said, I am the Son of God?** *37* If I do not the works of my Father, believe me not. *38* **But if I do, though ye believe not me, believe the works:** that ye may know, and believe, that **the Father is in me, and I in him** *(God and His Word).*"

Also, in **John 8:42**, the Lord Jesus said:

> "...If **God were your Father, ye would love me:** for **I proceeded forth** and came from God *(Jesus*

came out of God's mouth); **neither came I of myself, but he sent me.**"

It cannot be any clearer as to **where the Lord Jesus came from** — out of God's mouth! You must know for yourself that the **things written about the Lord Jesus in the Bible are not lies, hoaxes or something that Christians made up.** They are the true Words of the Almighty, the only True God who created the Heavens and the earth and who owns all souls.

I Watched the Word of God in the Bible Transformed into God Himself

*I had an opportunity **to see for myself** that **God and His Word** (both the **written Word** in the Bible and the **Lord Jesus Christ**) **are One**. God the Father had told me that **He and His Word are One** during one of **His visitations with me**.*

*One day, I was reading **Proverbs 11:30** in the **Bible** that says, "…**He that Winneth Souls is Wise**," and to my amazement, the 'W' in **wise leaped off** the **pages of my Bible** and **it began to transform into a Face**; **God's Face** and it **became the Full Person of God the Father!** **He placed His right index finger on His chin** and with **a broad smile said to me**, "**I told you that I and My Word are One**."*

*This was **not a vision** or **a dream** but something that happened in broad daylight right before my eyes as I was reading my Bible. **I mean, God the Father was sprawled out across the open pages of my Bible and smiling at me!** I saw for myself that **God and His Word are one; that the Lord Jesus is the Word that came out of God's Mouth.** There is no lie or mistake about it.*

This is why you must not hold on to your past Islamic unbelief but turn to the Lord Jesus Christ for the salvation of your soul. He will save you when you turn to Him and make Him your Lord forever. The alternative is hell for all those who reject Him.

The Steps and Message of Salvation

Since you have been a Muslim, I know that you have never made the Lord Jesus your Savior but you can do it right now. To receive the Lord Jesus as your Savior, you must first believe that the Lord Jesus Christ is the Son of the Living God and then, believe the Good News of the Word of God in **John 3:16-18:**

> "For God so loved the world, that he gave his only begotten Son, that whosoever believeth in him should not perish, but have everlasting life. For God sent not his Son into the world to condemn the world; but that the world through him might be saved. 18 He that believeth on him is not condemned: but he that believeth not is condemned already, because he hath not believed in the name of the only begotten Son of God."

You must also believe that **the Lord Jesus is the only way that you can get to God in Heaven** as stated in **Romans 10:9-10:**

> "That if thou shalt **confess with thy mouth the Lord Jesus,** and **shalt believe in thine heart that God hath raised him from the dead,** thou **shalt be saved.** 10 For **with the heart man believeth unto righteousness;** and with **the mouth confession is made unto salvation."**

Pray this Prayer below **aloud** if you **believe** what is written in the Scriptures above:

The Prayer of Salvation

"Father God, in the name of the Lord Jesus, **I come to You now because I believe that Jesus Christ is Your Son and that He is God.** I choose Your Word that is written in the Bible as the only Word of God. **Father, I renounce my membership in the Islamic faith and all its beliefs, doctrines, rituals, its prayers and worship.**

I also believe that He came into the World in the flesh and that He was crucified on the Cross for my sins. He died on the Cross for my sins and was buried but on the third day, You raised Him from the dead. Today, I confess it with my mouth and I believe it in my heart.

Lord Jesus, I repent of all my sins and I ask You to forgive me all my sins and wash me with Your blood. Please, **come into my heart and be my Lord** for I surrender to Your Lordship this day and forever. Give me Your Eternal Life for I declare that I belong to You from now on.

Also, I **ask You to give me Your Holy Spirit** to keep me in Your will, teach me the Bible, lead and protect me. I choose to do only those things that please You from now on. Father, I believe that You heard me and that I am now your child. Thank You for giving me Your Son and Your Holy Spirit. I receive them in the name of the Lord Jesus; Amen."

Get a copy of the New King James (*NKJ*) version of the Bible and read it instead of the Koran.

Chapter 14
Flee from the Roman Catholic Church

The Pagan Origin of the Roman Catholic Church

The Roman Catholic Church is a 'Pit' whose members that are now Left Behind need to rethink and run away from. It is and has always been a pagan institution with pagan practices and rituals. The Roman Catholic Church which means, 'Universal Church' *(catholic)*, is the '**Remnant of Emperor worship' of Rome.** To trace the origin of the Catholic institution, we begin with **Julius Caesar.** When he briefly **became Emperor**, he took to Himself, the title of **Pontifex Maximus**; he usurped the position of the pagan Chief High Priest and **he began to preside over all pagan religious activities in Rome.**

His fellow Senators were not pleased with him for this because he elevated himself above them. As a result, they plotted and killed him in the Senate building. After his death, his adopted son Octavius succeeded him as Emperor and he **declared Julius Caesar a 'god**.' Octavius renamed himself as Emperor Augustus and also conferred upon himself the title of **Pontifex Maximus**. He declared himself to be the '**son of a god,**' he demanded to be worshipped and the **Romans began to worship him as a god!** Thereafter, **all the Roman Emperors were venerated as gods and they received worship**.

How the Pope Got His Title

After the fall of the Roman Empire, the '**Bishop of Rome'** as the Pope was previously called, **stepped up to assume the leadership of all religious activities** *(paganism mixed with church worship)* in Rome because he was already functioning under the emperors as a religious leader. For instance, most people are not aware that the title of the **Pope, Pontifex Maximus** was the name of the **Chief Pagan High Priest** who **presided over all pagan religious colleges and practices** in Rome. The Bishop of Rome then enlarged his '**self-proclaimed** role of **Pontifex Maximus'** which means **Supreme Pontiff** or simply referred to as Pontiff or Pope! This pagan title with layers of clothing, rituals and kissing of the Pope's ring are still practiced daily by the priests and Pope of the Roman Catholic Church. They are all relics of emperor worship.

When the '**Bishop of Rome'** enlarged his office and assumed the title of Pontifex Maximus *(Supreme Priest or Chief Priest)* over the other Bishops, **the Bishop over Greece and the Bishop over Eastern Europe chose to hold onto the traditional views of the Bible.** Therefore, they broke away in protest of the 'Bishop of Rome' and they became Orthodox! Meaning that they chose the traditional biblical views but they too had been tainted with the pagan rituals under the Roman Emperors.

The Evil Fruits of the Roman Catholic Church

As you have just read above, **the Roman Catholic Church is not from the Lord Jesus Christ but a relic of the fallen Roman Empire.** The Pope occupies the 'Vacated Seat' of the last Roman emperor and he acts in the ways the Roman emperors did. From what you are going to read in the following subtitles, you will see its evil fruits from the day it was created. The Roman Catholic Church proves what the Lord Jesus said in **Matthew 7:16-20** that a corrupt tree cannot bring forth good fruit:

> "**Ye shall know them by their fruits.** Do men gather grapes of thorns, or figs of thistles? 17 Even so **every good tree bringeth forth good fruit; but a corrupt tree bringeth forth evil fruit.** 18 A good tree cannot bring forth evil fruit, **neither can a corrupt tree bring forth good fruit.** 19 Every tree that bringeth not forth good fruit is hewn down, and cast into the fire. 20 Wherefore by their fruits ye shall know them.**"

The evil fruits of the Roman Catholic Church are outlined in the following subjects in the subtitles below. **After reading** them, you will have no choice but to flee if you want to avoid hell and spend eternity with God the Father and the Lord Jesus Christ in Heaven.

Open Pagan Worship of Mithra

The Roman Catholic Church **abdicated the faith that is in the Lord Jesus Christ** centuries ago and instead, began to engage in the open worship of **Mithra; the Roman Sun-god**. In ancient Rome, **Mithra was worshiped by its priests who conducted the 'Mass;'** a daily ritual to honor him. They had what they called, **'Vestal Virgins' of young males and females who took the 'Vow of Celibacy;'** *(not getting married)* to devote themselves solely to Mithra.

The Bishop of Rome brought these forms of pagan worship and its rituals into the Roman Catholic Church when he made himself Pontifex Maximus or the Chief Priest. He also imported celebration of **Mass** and the **'Vestal Virgins'** into the church; they are now serving as **Priests and Nuns with vows of celibacy**!

Also, every **Mass** *(Mithra worship)* that is celebrated daily in the Roman Catholic Church is dedicated to a 'dead saint.' The truth is, saying Mass to 'dead saints' for spiritual intervention, **bypasses God the Father and the Lord Jesus** who will not share their glory with a dead saint. As a result, **this form of worship is a satanic ritual.**

Worship of Idols or Graven Images

Outside of every Roman Catholic Church are ceramic images or figures of 'Christ,' the 'Virgin Mary,' any dead saints you can think of and they are all venerated by 'faithful members.' Upon entering any Roman Catholic Church, you are again confronted with more graven or ceramic images and members are **required to bow** to the huge graven image of 'Christ' prominently displayed before you at the Alter. To take it a step further, some of their members go to **light candles to some of these images in prayer.**

Years ago, **Pope Pius IX crowned a giant size graven image of the 'Virgin Mary'** at the ancient 'Roman Column' in Rome. He bestowed upon this graven image the title of the *'Column of Immaculate Conception.'* **Contrary to what is written in the Bible that "all have sinned," Pope Pius IX** declared that, **"Mary was born without the Adamic or the Original sin!"** This is a <u>colossal heresy</u> because the <u>Lord Jesus is the only human being that was born without sin because God's Word conceived Him.</u> Pope Pius IX's action negates the works of Christ on the Cross for Mary's soul.

Upon visiting the country of Chile in 2018, Pope Francis also crowned the statue of the **'Virgin Mary'** as the **'<u>Mother of Chile</u>.'** Along with this lunacy, there are giant images of the 'Virgin Mary' all over the world that are venerated by members of the Roman Catholic Church. Some of these statues have **been seen to bleed and shed tears** as the <u>devil sends his demons into them</u> to do these things so that people will continue to venerate them all over the world without knowing that **they are worshipping the devil!**

The reason the devil can do this is because God said in His word that we are not to make graven images *(idols)*, bring them to our homes or bow down to them to worship them — **Exodus 20:3-5**:

> **"You shall have no other gods before me.** 4 **"You shall not make for yourself an image in the form of anything in heaven above or on the earth beneath or in the waters below.** 5 <u>**You shall not bow down to them or worship them**</u>; for I, the Lord your God, am a jealous God, punishing the children for the sin of the parents to the third and fourth generation of those who hate me."

Here is what the Word of God says about Christians having fellowship with idols in **2 Corinthians 6:14-18**:

> **<u>"Be ye not unequally yoked together with unbelievers</u>: for what fellowship hath righteousness**

with unrighteousness? and what communion hath light with darkness? 15 And what concord hath Christ with Belial? or what part hath he that believeth with an infidel? 16 And what agreement hath the temple of God with idols? for ye are the temple of the living God;

as God hath said, I will dwell in them, and walk in them; and I will be their God, and they shall be my people. 17 **Wherefore come out from among them, and be ye separate,** saith the Lord, and touch not the unclean thing; and I will receive you, 18 And will be a Father unto you, and ye shall be my sons and daughters, saith the Lord Almighty."

Yet, a lot of Roman Catholic Church members who make **annual pilgrimages to visit and venerate these statues are not illiterate but their Church conditioned them not to read the Bible.** This keeps them ignorant of what God's Word says in the Bible.

The Counting of the Rosary Beads

The counting of the Rosary Beads is based on what the Roman Catholic Church believed was an '**Apparition**' or a supernatural appearance of a so-called '**Virgin Mary**' who gave the instructions to '**Pray the Rosary Beads**'! In **1569**, a **Papal Bull** *(formal Papal decree or document)* **established praying with the Rosary Beads** and gave it the title of, **Our Lady of the Rosary.** As a result, when **Pope Pius V** wanted to gain victory in **his war of 1571**, he requested Catholics in Europe to pray with the Rosary Beads.

Today, the Roman Catholic Church's counting of the Rosary Beads is practiced all over the world and it is all about the 'Virgin Mary;' it is really the work of the deceptive demon known as the '**Queen of Heaven**.' **Since counting of the Rosary Beads is not from God, it does not acknowledge the Lord Jesus who is the only Mediator between God and**

man. By design, members are taught to pray with the Beads as follows: **6 beads are for <u>prayer</u> to God the Father, 53 beads** *(3 initial beads plus 5 sets of 10 beads)* **are for <u>prayers</u> to the 'Virgin Mary;' a.k.a. the Queen of Heaven and <u>the Lord Jesus</u> is nowhere to be found in the Rosary Beads!**

This counting of the Rosary beads by Catholics is identical to the **Buddhists and Muslims'** counting of beads in their prayers. Again, the <u>Apparition</u> *(lying vision)* leading to its use was **not from God because Christians are told by God not to engage in <u>Necromancy</u>** *(talking to the dead)* as the evil spirit behind its use suggests; praying to Mary. It is demonic, not of God and should be avoided by all Christians.

Forbidding Members from Reading the Bible

The Roman Catholic Church has a **history of forbidding its members from reading the Bible and those who were found with a Bible were burnt at the stake as heretics!** As a result, the **<u>Roman Catholic Church has killed more faithful Bible believers in Jesus Christ than any other institution on earth.</u>** For example, when Martin Luther set out to expose the atrocities of the Pope and Johannes Gutenberg invented the Printing Press, they made copies of the Printed Bible available to people in Europe.

The Roman Catholic Popes, bishops and priests set out to squash all those who would live by what is written in the Bible. They **hunted down Christians who possessed a copy of the Bible and brought charges of heresy against them for going against the false doctrines of the Roman Catholic Church**. They were given an opportunity to Renounce what is written in the Bible and believe the church doctrines instead. **Whoever refused to renounce what is written in the Bible, was burnt at the stake as a heretic against the church.**

Also, many priests and bishops were known for placing a statue of the 'Virgin Mary' in a public place and set spies to watch all those who **passed by without venerating it**; these people were noted. They were then **summoned before the church and told to venerate the statue and when any of them refused, he or she was marched to the stake and burnt as a heretic** against the church! You have seen so far, how evil the Roman Catholic Church has been to God's True Believers and how **it has always been about pagan worship and doctrines of man.**

This evil practice of killing Christians for believing what is written in the Bible lasted for **hundreds of years and many Bible believing Christians lost their lives.** This should leave no doubt in your mind that this **relic of the Roman Empire** known as the **Roman Catholic Church** is an **antichrist institution** that exports paganism to their members all over the world and that hates the Word of God.

As a result of the serious damage this church has done, members of the Roman Catholic Church to this day have a very poor understanding of the Word of God in the Bible. This is why you should not be surprised to see many of them left behind after Rapture.

The False Doctrines of the Church

For your information, the Lord Jesus was known as the Angel of the Lord before He was Born through Mary. He appeared to Moses at the burning bush as such in **Exodus 3:1-2** and He was the one who led the children of Israel through the wilderness for 40 years:

> "Now Moses kept the flock of Jethro his father-in-law, the priest of Midian: and he led the flock to the backside of the desert, and came to the mountain of God, even to Horeb. 2 And the **angel of the Lord appeared unto him in a flame of fire out of the midst of a bush**: and he looked, and, behold, the bush burned with fire, and the bush was not consumed."

As everyone knows, He was crucified on the Cross once but the Roman Catholic Church crucifies Him at every communion.

1. The Doctrine of Transubstantiation

This is the heretical belief that every time they offer the **Sacrament of Holy Communion** *(the Eucharist)*, the **substance** of the **Bread** and the **Wine, miraculously turn into the Body and Blood of Jesus Christ.** By doing this, they crucify the Lord Jesus again and again during their Sacrament of Holy Communion; something that God hates.

This the very sin that Moses and Aaron committed that cost them the Promised Land. It is recorded in **Exodus 17:6** that when the children of Israel cried for water, God told Moses to **Smite the Rock** *(Jesus)* and water will come out of it:

> **"Behold, I** *(Jesus; the Rock)* **will stand before thee there Upon the Rock** in Horeb; and **thou shalt smite the rock,** and **there shall come water out of it**, that the people may drink. And Moses did so in the sight of the elders of Israel."

We are blessed by **the blow** that the Lord Jesus took for us on the Cross as the Rock, so **we are now commanded to speak to Him to receive God's blessings**. This is why the next time the children of Israel cried for water; God told Moses to **Speak to the Rock** but Moses in anger **Struck the Rock twice;** which **in God's sight was a very serious offense**. This is because Moses did not know that the **Rock was Christ who can only be crucified once** *(struck)* — **Numbers 20:8-12:**

> "Take the rod, and gather **thou** the assembly together, thou, and **Aaron** thy brother, and **speak ye unto the rock** before their eyes; and **it shall give forth his water** *(see that the Rock is a person?)* and **thou shalt bring forth to them water out of the rock**: so thou shalt give the congregation and their beasts drink. 9 And Moses took the rod from before the LORD, as he commanded him.

10 And Moses and Aaron gathered the congregation together before the rock, and he said unto them, **Hear now, ye rebels; must we fetch you water out of this rock?** 11 And **Moses lifted up his hand, and <u>with his rod he smote the rock twice:</u>** and the water came out abundantly, and the congregation drank, and their beasts also. 12 And the LORD spake unto Moses and Aaron**, because ye believed me not, to sanctify me in the eyes of the children of Israel, therefore ye shall not bring this congregation into the land which I have given them.**"

This act of trying to crucify the Lord Jesus Christ a second time is very displeasing to God but unfortunately, in the Roman Catholic's celebration of the Holy Communion, **Christ is crucified over and over again on a daily basis;** a grievous sin.

2. **The Vicar of Christ and the Infallibility of the Pope**
The Vicar of Christ means that the Pope has replaced Christ; it is the false doctrine that '**usurps Christ's Seat and Authority' over His Church**. This heretical doctrine claims that the Pope is the Head of the Church and that he *(the Pope)* sits as the Vicar of Christ; **meaning that the Pope has taken the position of Christ with all divine authority! <u>Therefore, instead of Christ, the Pope is the head of the Roman Catholic Church.</u>** The Lord Jesus was essentially kicked out of the Roman Catholic Church; though they speak about Him, they do not want Him as the head of the church.

In addition to this, there is the **belief that the Pope is infallible in everything he says and does.** According to this false doctrine, **the Lord Jesus' Word to the Apostle Peter regarding the Rock on which He would build His Church, was handed down to the Pope. This exempts the Pope from the possibility of Error**! If this is not self-exaltation and hubris of the first order, I do not know what is.

Roman Catholic Pope(s) have conveniently appropriated to themselves the Lord Jesus' words in **Matthew 16:15-18** about Himself as the Rock. In the scripture which is quoted below, the Lord was speaking about the revelation Peter received from God about Jesus being the Christ; the Son of God:

"He saith unto them, <u>But whom say ye that I am?</u> *16* And Simon Peter answered and said, **<u>Thou art the Christ, the Son of the living God</u>**. *17* And Jesus answered and said unto him, **Blessed art thou, Simon Barjona: for flesh and blood hath not revealed it unto thee, but my Father which is in heaven.** *18* **And I say also unto thee, That thou art Peter** *(Pebble),* **and upon this Rock** *(upon this revelation Peter received from God about the Lord)* **<u>I will build my church;</u>** **and the gates of hell shall not prevail against it.**"

Be it known to everyone that Peter means a pebble and not a rock. **The Lord Jesus Christ has always been and He will always be the Rock upon which God's Church is built** and not the Pope. **No one dared usurp the Lord's authority but the Pope(s) of the Roman Catholic Church <u>and also the person who sits as the Head of the Church of England since Henry XIII!</u>** All those who have occupied these two seats have usurped Christ's Authority over His Church and they have been doing it for centuries to their detriment. **If you are wise, you will get away from both of these churches lest they make you a 'son of perdition.'**

3. **The Doctrine of Excommunication**

It is another false belief in the Roman Catholic Church that the Pope or a bishop can officially exclude a person from participating in Holy Sacrament and from going to Heaven. The person can only be restored if he or she appeals to the Pope and is granted a pardon. This violates what the Lord Jesus said in **John 6:37:**

"All that the Father giveth me shall come to me; and **<u>him that cometh to me I will in no wise cast out.</u>**"

The most prominent example of the Roman Catholic Church's act of Excommunication, is **John Wycliffe**. The church excommunicated John Wycliffe and **burnt him at the stake along with his manuscripts for translating the Bible from Latin to English so that everyone can read God's Word for themselves.** The church was not satisfied with Wycliffe's death at the stake because, years later, Pope Martin V acting as though he was God, had **Wycliffe's bones dug up, burned, ground the ashes to powder, cursed and excommunicated Wycliffe to hell** before having the ashes thrown into the river. I believe that today, it is Wycliffe who is looking from heaven at the Pope(s) as they are burning in hell.

The Pope(s) and Bishops believed Wycliffe's crime was very serious because before his time, every Pope was able to **keep people from reading the Bible so that they will remain ignorant of God's Word**. This enabled the Pope(s) to use their self-appointed authority to exert unchallenged control over monarchies and all the people in Europe. In addition to this, they were getting very rich from charging the people money for atonement of their sins and **the people being ignorant of the Word of God written in Latin, were eager to pay**. They did not know that salvation is free just by asking and that all anyone needs is faith in Christ.

The Pope(s) had taught the people to believe that paying money for forgiveness of sins was the <u>way to receive salvation from God</u>! This practice went on unchallenged for years until John Wycliffe translated the Bible into English for every person who can read to know what the Bible says. This aroused the anger of the Pope and bishops and they hunted Wycliffe for years until they successfully entrapped him using one of his friends. After they burnt him at the stake, they sought to obtain every copy of the Wycliffe Bible to burn them or so they thought but the King of England had one and so did a few other people.

Some years later, **Martin Luther adopted Wycliffe's translation of the Bible**; he had been studying Wycliffe's work. **He then, set out to expose the Pope and the church as a money-making institution that perverted the Word of God.** Thanks be to God, with the help of Johannes Guttenberg and his Printing Press, they succeeded in making copies of the Bible available to lay people. **A testimony that although Wycliffe was killed by the Roman Catholic Church, they could not destroy his work!**

3. **The Belief in Purgatory**
   Another false doctrine of the Roman Catholic Church is the **belief in the existence of Purgatory. They believe this place to be a section of hell where people do penance; a voluntary self-inflicted punishment to pay for sins.** This fallacy teaches that when their members die, they go first to Purgatory where they pay for their sins and wrong doings so that they can become worthy of Heaven.

   You cannot make up this type of fallacy even if you try, but in the Roman Catholic Church, it is a doctrine that has been sanctioned by every Pope for centuries. The truth is that **this is a man-made doctrine that gives false-hope to all Catholics that after death, they can go to this non-existent place and be purified for a life in Heaven.** The truth is, God's Word in **Hebrews 9:27** says:

   "And as **it is appointed unto men once to die, but after this the judgment.**"

   The Lord Jesus' teaching is that **those who believed in Him and lived according to His Word, will go straight to Heaven while those who do not believe in Him and lived contrary to His Word, will go directly to hell forever.** Therefore, be it known to all Catholics that God does not have a **waiting place of purification for the dead; it is either Heaven or hell upon death.**

Christianization of Pagan Feasts
The **Emperor Constantine** of Rome was a pagan but when he **converted to Christianity, he did not abandon his pagan**

beliefs. Instead, he used his position as **Pontifex Maximus** or Supreme Priest to incorporate all the religions in Rome under him. He established very grandiose Cathedral Church buildings with Steeples *(the pagan Tower of Babel)* on top of them so that the **Pagans can also feel comfortable when they enter**; these buildings were for both Christians and Pagans.

Emperor Constantine mandated that every house of worship should be according to his prototype and he ordained that December 25 be celebrated as the birthday of the Roman sun-god Mithra. Upon becoming a Christian, he mandated the co-celebration of Mithra's birthday with 'Christ's birthday;' calling it **Christ-Mass** *(Christ and Mithra)*. The following are Pagan Feasts that are supposedly 'Christianized' by the Roman Catholic Church:

1. Christmas

When the Roman Catholic Church was created by the bishop of Rome, **he saw nothing wrong with Constantine's day of worshipping Christ and Mithra together.** He embraced and adopted it in the church and it has since spread all over the world. **The devil has totally reclaimed it as his pagan feast that it was from the beginning.** This is why today; you are not **allowed to mention Jesus' Name in the media even at Christmas for fear that you might offend someone.**

As you can see in recent years, Christmas songs are no longer about Jesus but about Santa Clause, reindeers, and other secular topics. Meaning that **Christmas is now purely a pagan celebration with Mithra traditions of decorated evergreen trees** *(pagan tree)*, **sun-god lights, caroling, giving of gifts and meals.**

2. Halloween Celebration

The Roman Catholic Church also brought the pagan celebration of Halloween into the church and Catholics all over the world began to celebrate it. Their belief was that the church was **reclaiming the pagan Halloween for**

Christ. They established the tradition of **celebrating Mass for Catholic 'dead saints' the night before Halloween and they call it 'Night of Light;'** an oxymoron.

The fact is that Halloween is another pagan feast that the Roman Catholic Church institution supposedly '**Christianized' but how can you 'Christianize' the celebration of <u>death</u> and the <u>dead</u> in the Church of Jesus Christ when <u>Christ came to destroy the devil and his power of death?</u>**

> "Forasmuch then as the children are partakers of flesh and blood, he (*Jesus*) also himself likewise took part of the same; **that through death he might destroy him that had the power of death, that is, the devil**" (Hebrews 2:14).

No matter what the Roman Catholic Church institution tells the world, **Halloween remains a demonic 'worship of the Dead and Death.'** For years, Hollywood and major corporations promoted it because it generates profits from horror films, sales of costumes, candies, pumpkins and decorations. **Stay away from its celebration if you profess to belong to Christ.**

3. Easter Celebration

Easter is the Sumerian worship of their goddess Inanna widely known by her Babylonian name as Ishtar and it dates back to 2100 BC. She was known in the land of **Canaan as Astarte or Ashtoreth** while the **Greek referred to her as Aphrodite and Venus**. They regarded her as the goddess of love and pleasure and she was worshipped with sexual pleasures and perversions.

According to church history, when the Roman Catholic Church identified the spot in Jerusalem where the **Temple of Aphrodite was erected by the Romans, they tore it down and erected a church** there. This church is still very much in use today and it is called, '**The Church of the Holy Sepulcher**.' Although this church replaced the Temple of Aphrodite, it continued the tradition of Ishtar or Easter *(anglicized)* which then spread to the rest of the Catholic Churches and all over the world. As you can see, **Easter is based on a pagan 'fertility worship' of a pagan deity.** No Christian should celebrate it.

If you noticed, all the Pagan Feasts that were 'supposedly' reclaimed or 'Christianized' by the Roman Catholic Church, **have gone back to their pagan roots because, they were never from God.** The only group profiting from the celebrations of these feasts are the department stores that make millions of dollars from the sale of the items used in their celebrations.

As for the devil, **he uses these feasts to receive 'proxy' or 'representative' worship** from those celebrating them. Meanwhile, **all who celebrate them leave themselves wide-open to all sorts of demonic afflictions.**

More Reasons Why You Should Flee the Roman Catholic Church

If the pagan history and practices in the above subtitles were not enough to make you run for your life from the Roman Catholic Church, here are **Heaven or hell reasons why you should**.

1. Who You Belong to
   Roman Catholic Church members pledge their allegiance to the Church <u>instead of</u> the Lord Jesus Christ. As a Born Again Christian, have you ever tried to speak to a Roman Catholic Church member about Jesus Christ? When you try to tell them about the Gospel of Christ, their response to you is, "I am Catholic." By their confession, they belong to the Roman Catholic Church and not to Jesus Christ and as a result, He could not take many of them at Rapture.

   If as a Catholic you were left behind after Rapture occurred, know that you must belong to the Lord Jesus Christ in order to get saved and get into His Heaven. <u>You cannot belong to the Roman Catholic Church and hope to get into Heaven because it is a pagan institution</u>. The

Roman Catholic Church **does not point people to Christ but to pagan practices, demonic worship of the Queen of Heaven** *(Virgin Mary)* **and the Pope as the source of atonement of sins.** You cannot have the Pope or a priest forgive you your sins and **bypass the Lord Jesus.**

2. **Avoiding the 'Mind-Binding' Occult Spirits in the Church**
   While preaching the Gospel, I once tried to tell a Roman Catholic Church member about her need to receive the salvation that is in Christ and her need to make Jesus her Lord until I lost my voice. To my amazement, whenever I thought that I had properly explained to her about her need for Christ, she responded that she was Catholic repeatedly!

   I went to the Lord because I lost my voice and I asked Him why almost all Catholic Church members seem to have the same response of "I am Catholic" to the Gospel and He told me that, **"There is a mind-binding occult spirit in the Roman Catholic Church"** that does not allow its members to hear the Gospel even after talking to them for hours. I should know because **I was a Catholic Church member with the same response for years and no one could reach me with the Gospel until the Lord in a vision removed the fingers of this spirit that it had plunged into my ears.**

   The Lord did this on a Sunday at an evangelical church service and I was Born Again *(saved)* the following Tuesday! Because of the **paganism and the occult spirits** in the Roman Catholic Church, the members cannot pledge loyalty to any other entity *(even Christ)* because their minds have been bound by these spirits. **You will not be able to reject the Mark of the Beast if you remain in the Roman Catholic Church and if you receive the Mark, you will be damned forever.**

3. **The Pope Will Rise as the False Prophet**
   From what I have read in the Bible and as I discussed earlier, I have concluded that **the false prophet will be none other than the Roman Catholic Pope.** You do not want to be under him when he is **commanding the whole world to**

17

worship the Beast and take his Mark on their foreheads or on their right hands to become damned forever. If you choose to remain under the Pope, you will **not have the power to resist him because spiritually, you are his subject.** You will be under his spell that you cannot break.

For more information, you can read more about the **Pope as the false prophet** in the *Chapter* titled, *The Rise of the Antichrist and the False Prophet.*

Steps to Come Out of the Roman Catholic Church

To distance yourself from the Roman Catholic Church so it does not drag you to hell, you need to **renounce your membership, the doctrines or Catechisms,' heresy in its rituals and worship, idolatry of graven images or statues, worship of the 'Virgin Mary,' prayers to dead saints, etc.**

Pray this Prayer below **aloud** if you **believe** that the Lord Jesus died for your sins and want Him to be your Lord and Savior.

Prayer to Come out of the Roman Catholic Church and Make Jesus Your Lord

"Dear Heavenly Father, I come to You in the name of the Lord Jesus and **I repent of every sin that I have committed against You through my membership and adherence to the doctrines and rituals in the Roman Catholic Church**. I confess that it is against you that I sinned and I now want to get away from these sinful practices. Lord Jesus, I renounce my membership in the Roman Catholic Church and pledging my allegiance to the Church instead of You.

Lord, I ask You to please, forgive me all my sins; including the **Catholic doctrines or 'Catechisms'** *(including transubstantiation),* **the heresies in its worship services and rituals, the idolatry of graven images or statues and for seeking the intercession of dead saints on my behalf in my prayers. Lord, I repent of every prayer that I ever prayed to**

185

the 'Virgin Mary' as well as seeking prayers of absolution *(forgiveness of sins)* from Catholic priests at confession instead of coming directly to You.

I am so sorry for all these sins. Lord Jesus, cleanse me with Your Blood from all my sins; even every sin that I have committed since I came out of my mother's womb. **I repent of them all and I want to be Born Again by the Holy Spirit for I believe Lord, that You are the Son of God. I also believe You came into this world and died on the Cross for my sins and that You were buried but on the third day, God the Father raised You from the dead to give me eternal life.**

Please, Lord Jesus, wash me of my sins with Your blood and come into my heart and be my Lord and Savior. **Give me Your Eternal Life and baptize me with the Holy Spirit to keep me, teach me Your Word and guide me from now on.** Lord, I believe that You heard me and that I am now Born Again by Your Spirit. As such, I am now a child of the Living God in You. Father, I thank You for giving me Your Son and Your Holy Spirit and I receive them in the name of the Lord Jesus; Amen."

Chapter 15
To the Jehovah Witnesses Left Behind

Why You Were Left Behind

The Jehovah's Witnesses are not exempted from the people left behind after Rapture because they have so many false beliefs and doctrines. **Their first stumbling block is that they do not believe that the Lord Jesus is God and they out rightly reject the existence of the Holy Spirit.**

Without believing that **the Lord Jesus is the Son of God and therefore God, and by not receiving God's Gift of the Holy Spirit, there is no way for anyone who practices this faith to be a candidate for Rapture or Heaven.** Below are additional stumbling blocks.

Only the '144 thousand Jehovah's Witnesses' are Worthy of Heaven

Ironically, most members of the Jehovah's Witnesses Faith do not consider themselves worthy of Heaven but believe that only the **144 thousand in Revelation 14:3-5 are worthy to go to Heaven:**

> "And they sung as it were a new song before the throne, and before the four beasts, and the elders: and no man could learn that song but **the hundred and forty and four thousand, which were redeemed from the earth.** 4 These are they which were not defiled with women; for they are virgins.
>
> These are they which follow the Lamb whithersoever he goeth. **These were redeemed from among men, being the firstfruits unto God and to the Lamb.** 5 And in their mouth was found no guile: for they are without fault before the throne of God."

They totally ignore the scripture in **Revelation 7:4** that tells us that **the 144 thousand souls were Jewish believers of the Tribulation period:**

> "And I heard the number of them which were sealed: and there were **sealed an hundred and**

forty and four thousand of all the tribes of the children of Israel."

Now, how can anyone misinterpret or misread the above scripture? When you read it carefully, you will see that **it is talking about the Jews and not the Jehovah's Witnesses.** They appropriated this scripture above to themselves by believing that the 144 thousand it is talking about are their members. As a result, they **believe that only 144 thousand redeemed souls will go to Heaven from their congregations all over the earth**!

The Rest of Them Will 'Inherit' the Earth

According to their false doctrine, members not worthy to live in Heaven will "inherit the Earth." **Now, as a Jehovah's Witness who is left behind after Rapture, take a look at the earth you are now left in; does it look like a place for you to inherit?** For your information, **God will roll the earth up like a scroll** and **pour out His judgments** upon it — **Revelation 6:12-17:**

> "And I beheld when he had opened the sixth seal of *(God's Judgment)*, and, lo, there was **a great earthquake; and the sun became black as sackcloth of hair, and the moon became as blood;** 13 And **the stars of heaven fell unto the earth**, even as a fig tree casteth her untimely figs, when she is shaken of a mighty wind.
>
> 14 And **the Heaven Departed as a Scroll when it is Rolled Together; and every mountain and island were moved out of their places**. 15 And the kings of the earth, and the great men, and the rich men, and the chief captains, and the mighty men, and every bondman, and every free man, hid themselves in the dens and in the rocks of the mountains;
>
> 16 And **said to the mountains and rocks, Fall on us, and hide us from the face of him that sitteth on the throne, and from the wrath of the Lamb**: 17 **For the great day of his wrath is come;** and who shall be able to stand?"

188

You must be aware that according to **2 Peter 3:10-12, God is going burn the earth up with Fire** so, there will be nothing for you to inherit:

> "But the day of the Lord will come as a thief in the night; in the which *(Christ's Second Coming to judge the wicked)* **the heavens shall pass away with a great noise, and** <u>the elements shall melt with fervent heat, the earth also and the works that are therein shall be burned up.</u> *11* Seeing then that **all these things shall be dissolved**, what manner of persons ought ye to be in all holy conversation and godliness, *12* Looking for and hasting unto the coming of the day of God, **wherein the heavens being on fire shall be dissolved, and the elements shall melt with fervent heat?**"

You can see that God does not want the earth to remain in its present corrupt state; He will renovate it with fire. **This is why you must abandon the doctrine of inheriting the earth** <u>because when Christ comes to judge men's actions on earth, all those who rejected Him will be condemned to hell</u>.

Only the Righteous will Dwell on the New Earth

After God Renovates the Earth by Fire, only the **Righteous** who were **Redeemed by Jesus Christ** shall live in the '**New Earth**' as we see in **2 Peter 3:13:**

> "Nevertheless we *(believers in Jesus Christ)* according to his promise, **look for New Heavens and a New Earth, <u>wherein dwelleth Righteousness</u>.**"

Only those who allowed the Lord Jesus to wash away their unrighteousness and give them His own righteousness will qualify to live in the New Earth; this does not include the Jehovah's Witnesses' who rejected Him and the Holy Spirit. In **Revelation 21:27**, we are told that:

> "And **there shall in no wise enter into it** *(the 'New Jerusalem' brought to earth from Heaven)* **anything that**

**defileth, neither whatsoever worketh abomi-
nation, or maketh a lie** *(false doctrine):* **but they**
which are **written in the Lamb's book of life."**

To be written in the Lamb's (*Christ*) 'Book of Life,' you have to
belong to Him by making Him your Lord and Savior which is
something that the Jehovah Witnesses failed to do.

What I Saw at Jehovah's Witnesses Thanksgiving Communion Service

Some years before I came to Christ, I was **seeking understanding about a dream in which the Lord Jesus appeared
to me and He was not pleased with me.** Therefore, I spoke
to a Jehovah's Witness lady because I thought, since they go
door-to-door witnessing to people, they might be able to help
me to understand my dream. She took me to their Kingdom
Hall service and not long after that, I went with her to their
'Thanksgiving Communion Service.'

At the service, she told me not to drink the wine or eat
the bread when it is passed down to me. To my surprise, **no
one present at the service drank the wine or ate the bread** of
the Communion elements. As I watched, I could not wait to
find out why and they later informed me that, **"No one in the
assembly that night was worthy to eat the bread or drink the
wine but only the 144 thousand!"**

When they saw my surprise, **they told me that there
were two 'worthy people' in this particular congregation
that are counted among the 144 thousand** and I wanted to
know why they did not take part in the communion service.
According to them, **one was in the hospital and the other
one was sick at home.** I told them that for being the only two
people who are 'worthy,' in their congregation, they do not
seem to being doing well.

Although **I was not yet Born Again,** *(saved by Jesus)* and
did not yet **know the Bible,** I knew that this doctrine was
wrong. To make matters worse, when I asked the elders

about my dream, they informed me that, "**God does not talk to people in dreams or visions anymore and that my dream was from the devil.**" I tried to tell them that I had always seen the Lord Jesus in dreams since I was young but this dream was the only one in which He was angry with me but they insisted that it was from the devil. As a result, I told the lady not to contact me anymore and that I did not want anything to do with them.

It is Time for You to Repent

As a left behind Jehovah's Witness, you must rethink the false doctrine of the Jehovah's Witnesses that made you to miss Rapture. **You now need to choose the Lord Jesus; the Son of God and God who came in the human flesh as your Savior.** This is the only way that you can be saved **even if the forces of the antichrist kill your human body. Know that if you continue to believe in the false doctrines of the Jehovah's Witnesses, you will surely go to hell when you die**.

Ditch your former Jehovah's Witness's Bible with its **wrong interpretations and get a New King James Bible** *(NKJ)* because it is easier to read than the regular **King James Bible** but if you can read the regular King James version, it is preferable. Find out **the correct teaching of Christ in it and believe the '<u>Real</u> Good News' of the Gospel of Jesus Christ the Son of God.** Before you put this book down, **<u>ask Him to be your Lord and Savior</u> because He is the only way to Heaven.**

The Steps and Message of Salvation

To receive the Lord Jesus as your Savior, you must **believe the Real Good News** of the Word of God in **John 3:16-18:**

> **"For God so loved the world, that he gave his only begotten Son, that whosoever believeth in him should not perish, but have everlasting life.** For God sent not his Son into the world to condemn the world; but that the world through him might be saved. *18* **He that believeth on him is not condemned: but <u>he that believeth not is</u>**

<u>condemned already</u>, because he hath not believed in the name of the only begotten Son of God."

You must also believe that **the Lord Jesus is the Only Way** that you can get to God in Heaven as stated in **Romans 10:9-10:**

"That if thou shalt **confess with thy mouth the Lord Jesus,** and **shalt believe in thine heart that God hath raised him from the dead,** thou **shalt be saved.** *10* For with **the heart man believeth unto righteousness;** and with **the mouth confession is made unto salvation.**"

Pray this Prayer below **aloud if you believe** what is written in the Scriptures above:

The Prayer of Salvation

"**Father, in the name of the Lord Jesus,** I come to you because **I now believe that Jesus Christ is Your Son and that He is God. I believe that He came into the world in the flesh and that He was crucified on the Cross for my sins. He died on the Cross for my sins and was buried but on the third day, You raised Him from the dead.** Today, I confess it with my mouth and I believe it in my heart.

Lord Jesus, **I renounce my membership in the Jehovah's Witness organization and all its false beliefs and doctrines. I repent of all my sins and I ask You to forgive me and wash me with Your blood from all my sins.** Please, come into my heart and be my Lord for I surrender to Your Lordship this day and forever. Give me Your Eternal Life for I declare that I belong to You from now on.

Also, **I ask You to give me Your Holy Spirit** to keep me in Your will, teach me the Bible, lead and protect me. I choose to do only those things that please You from now on. Father, I believe that You heard me and that I am now your child. Thank You for giving me Your Son and Your Holy Spirit. I receive them in the name of the Lord Jesus; Amen."

Chapter 16
To Mormons or LDS Members Left Behind

The Mormon' Foundation and Narratives

The Mormon Church whose members are commonly referred to as Latter Day Saints or LDS and its narratives from an 18-year-old Joseph Smith was questionable from the very beginning. Smith claimed to have been visited by an Angel called **Moroni** and that the angel gave him 'Seven Gold Tablets.' I believe the name of the angel Moroni should remind you of the demoniac called Legion because he too did not hide his name but told the Lord Jesus that he was called Legion. Here you can see that demons sometimes tell you their name as revealed in **Mark 5:8-9:**

> "For he said unto him, Come out of the man, thou unclean spirit. 9 And he asked him, What is thy name? And he answered, saying, My name is Legion: for we are many."

No offense intended, but I tell you that Joseph Smith was not discerning of this demonic spirit. The 'Seven Gold Tablets' that Smith received from this so-called angel was the devil's evil plot against his soul and the souls of millions of Mormons. Please exercise your God-given common sense and receive Christ as your Savior; stop following the Moroni spirit. Smith made the mistake of authenticating and 'deciphering' the two tablets that only he saw and he fell into the devil's trap. With the devil's inspiration, he came up with a 'New Religion' and he then wrote the 'Book of Mormon' to support this newly founded religion!

Furthermore, **Smith did not believe that the Bible contains all the knowledge that everyone needs about God so he claimed that his revelation in the 'Book of Mormon' was the completion the Bible needed.** Also, contrary to the Lord Jesus' Words *(John 4:24)* that **God is a Spirit** and the biblical teaching that **God is not a man** *(Numbers 23:19)*, Smith believed that God the Father was once a man and as such has a **'human body.'** In addition, **he said that there is no Trinity** (God the Father, God the Son and God the Holy Ghost). The problem was that Smith was a very charismatic person and he was able to sell his new false religion to the local farmers having been the son of a farmer himself.

The Reformed or New LDS

Over the years, Mormonism with its **polygamous practice faced persecution** but a segment of them were able to **reform their polygamous practice, rebranded themselves and gained many followers.** According to their published articles, they claimed to boast of **about 16 million members** worldwide. Nevertheless, **they all still adhere to their other false Mormon beliefs.**

Unfortunately, **all those who strictly adhered to the false narratives** written in Joseph Smith's **'Book of Mormon' and its doctrines, now find themselves left behind in a very wicked world with no escape route.**

Not Too Late for LDS Members to Come to Jesus

If you are one of these people and you need hope for your soul, I want you to know that **it is not too late for you to come to the Lord Jesus for the salvation of your soul.** However, **it is time for you to renounce the false Mormon faith, its beliefs and run to the Lord Jesus.** He alone is the **Savior of the World** and **He is the only hope** of every man — **1 Timothy 1:1:**

> "Paul, an apostle of Jesus Christ by the commandment of **God our Saviour,** and **Lord Jesus Christ, which is our hope**."

Your being left behind testifies that you did not believe in Christ nor did you make Him your Lord and Savior. At Rapture, He was obligated to take with Him only those who believed in Him and walked with Him faithfully. You can still be one of them because **He is coming back again 7 years after**

<u>Rapture to rule the world</u>. The whole world will see Him and **all those who rejected Him during the Time of Tribulation** (*7 years*) **will have an** <u>eternity</u> **of regrets in hell.**

Now is the time for you to believe in the Lord Jesus Christ, repent of your sins, ask Him to forgive you all your sins and invite Him to come into your heart as your Savoir. God the Father sent the Lord Jesus Christ to the earth to save all humanity so **ask Him to save you now before you put this book down.**

The Steps and Message of Salvation

To receive the Lord Jesus as your Savior, first, you must **believe the Good News** of the Word of God in **John 3:16-18:**

> **"For God so loved the world, that he gave his only begotten Son, that whosoever believeth in him should not perish, but have everlasting life.** For God sent not his Son into the world to condemn the world; but that the world through him might be saved. *18* **He that believeth on him is not condemned: but** <u>he that believeth not is condemned already</u>, because he hath not believed in the name of the only begotten Son of God."

You must also believe that **the Lord Jesus is the Only Way** that you can get to God in Heaven as stated in **Romans 10:9-10:**

> "That if thou shalt **confess with thy mouth the Lord Jesus,** and **shalt believe in thine heart that God hath raised him from the dead,** thou **shalt be saved.** *10* For **with the heart man believeth unto righteousness;** and with **the mouth confession is made unto salvation."**

Pray the Prayer below **aloud** if you **believe** what is written in the Scriptures above:

The Prayer of Salvation

"Father, in the name of the Lord Jesus, I come to You because **I believe that Jesus Christ is Your Son whom You sent to save me. I believe that He came into the world in the flesh and that He was crucified on the Cross for my sins. He died on the Cross for my sins, was buried but on the third day and You raised Him from the dead.** Today, I confess it with my mouth and I believe it in my heart.

Lord Jesus, I renounce my membership in Mormonism or LDS and all my previous beliefs in their doctrines. **I repent of all my sins and I ask that You forgive me and wash me with Your blood.** Come into my heart and be my Lord for I surrender to Your Lordship this day and forever. Please, give me your Eternal Life for I declare that I belong to You from now on.

Also, **I ask You to give me Your Holy Spirit** to keep me in Your will, teach me the Bible, lead and protect me. I choose to do only those things that please You from now on. Father, I believe that You heard me and that I am now your child. Thank You for giving me Your Son and Your Holy Spirit; I receive them in the name of the Lord Jesus; Amen."

Chapter 17
To Buddhists, Hindus and Other Religions

Common Denominator of all Those Left Behind

As you are aware by now, **no Buddhist, Hindu, Occultist, practitioners of other religions were taken during Rapture.** This is not by accident because the Lord Jesus only came to take 'His own away;' meaning, those who trusted and walked with Him faithfully.

I want you to know that sin is the common denominator of all the people that were left behind after Rapture. **The Lord Jesus paid for the sin of the whole world but millions and billions of people refused to come to Him to have their sins forgiven. Instead, many insisted on holding onto their family or national religion without any interest in Jesus Christ.** What is sad about this is that, the Lord Jesus is the only way that any human being can get to God; He is the only way that God provided for us all.

What the Occurrence of Rapture Should Prove to You

The occurrence of Rapture, your missing babies and friends should prove to you that there is only One God (Elohim; the God of the Bible) and that **He alone can save those who come to Him by His Son; Jesus Christ. Although you did not believe in Him, your very little innocent babies were taken by Him because they have not yet reached the age to choose not to belong to Him.** You as their parent may have chosen not to belong to Christ or follow Him but **your babies have not**. Until your babies grow up and you teach them to reject Him by dragging them into your religion, they belong to Him; He created them.

Although **you may have chosen not to follow the Lord Jesus but to practice a different religion from Christianity,** what you did not know is that there is **only One God** as revealed **in His Word in the Bible**. It is this Almighty God in the Bible that created the Heavens, the earth and everything in them. You now need to get to know Him because what **He declares about Himself in Isaiah 43:10-13** <u>directly affects you</u>:

> "Ye are my witnesses *(believers)*, **saith the LORD, and my servant whom I have chosen: that ye may know and believe me, and <u>understand that I am he</u>** *(God):* **<u>before me there was no God formed, neither shall there be after me.</u>** *11* **I, even I, am the LORD; and <u>beside me there is no saviour</u>**.
>
> *12* I have declared, and have saved, and I have shewed, when there was no strange god among you: **therefore ye are my witnesses, saith the LORD, that I am God.** *13* Yea, before the day was I am he; and **there is none that can deliver out of my hand: I will work, and who shall let it** *(meaning who can prevent me)*?"

He also declares the following in **Ezekiel 18:4:**

> "Behold, **all souls are mine** *(every human being);* **the soul of the father,** so also **the soul of the son is mine**: **<u>the soul that sinneth, it shall die</u>.**"

As you can see from His Word above, **your children were not really yours but His**! He created every human being **and we are all to live by His Word that is written in the Bible. Whoever does not live by God's Word is committing sin and if the person dies without going to Him to ask for forgiveness, the person shall go to hell.** God does not recognize any worship outside of the Bible. God again declared this about who He is in **Isaiah 46:8-10:**

> "Remember this, and shew yourselves men: bring it again to mind, O ye transgressors *(unbelievers in Him who do their own will)*. *9* Remember the former things of old: **for I am God, and there is none else; I am God, and there is none like me,** *10* Declaring the end from the beginning, and from ancient times the

things that are not yet done, **saying, <u>My counsel shall stand, and I will do all my pleasure</u>.**"

At **Rapture**, <u>He did His pleasure</u>; **saved faithful believers in Him and innocent babies all over the world.** As you are now a witness, **there were no <u>man-made gods</u> like Buddha, the millions of Hindu gods or any other entity that was able to prevent Him from taking out of the world what belongs to Him; including your babies!** Therefore, the Christian God of the Bible; the Almighty, is the Only God there is in the universe.

He created all souls; even the souls of your babies and dispatched them to earth for you to raise for Him. Knowing this now, it is not the time for you to blame Him but to thank Him and **<u>find out how you can get to know Him through His Son Jesus Christ</u> so that at the end of your life, you can be re-united with your babies and raptured loved ones.**

No Reincarnation

There is no reincarnation in His order of creation so that what you have been taught in Buddhism and Hinduism about reincarnation is wrong. As the Almighty God in the Bible designed it, you only get one chance in this world **to choose** where you will spend your eternity; Heaven or hell. If you choose to believe and faithfully follow the Lord Jesus Christ, you will go to Heaven even if you are killed on earth by unbelievers but **if you reject Christ, you will surely go to hell** because <u>the Lord Jesus is the only way to get to God</u> — **Acts 4:10-12:**

> "Be it known unto you all, and to all the people of Israel, that **by the name of Jesus Christ of Nazareth, whom ye crucified, whom God raised from the dead, even by him doth this man stand here before you whole.** *11* This is the stone which was set at nought of you builders, which is become the head of the corner.
>
> *12* **Neither is there salvation in any other: <u>for there is none other name under heaven given among men, whereby we must be saved</u>.**"

In **John 8:24**, the Lord Jesus told us emphatically that those who do not believe in Him shall die in their sins. Read His Words about those who refused to believe in Him:

> "I said therefore unto you, that ye shall die in your sins: **for if ye believe not that I am he, ye shall die in your sins.**"

These Words from the Lord's lips are to every human being on earth; we are to believe in Him and live but whoever does not believe in Him shall die in their sins and go to hell. No one is exempted because of their false religion; God commanded us all to follow Christ. Therefore, abandon Buddhism in order to save your soul.

Buddha Never Claimed to be God

Remember, **Buddha never claimed to be God** but <u>one who was still seeking</u> **and as for those who practice Hinduism; gods made with hands**, people worshiping man-made idols like the Greeks who worship the works of their hands will be damned. Be honest with yourself: **Is there a Buddha statue that was not made by a person?** The occurrence of Rapture should tell you that you need to seek the one True God which is the God of the Bible. **He is the only Creator of all human souls.**

No Provision for Cleansing Your Sins

<u>Neither Buddhism nor Hinduism has provision for the forgiveness of your sins</u>. This is because, **only the Almighty God of the Bible can wash away your sins by His own blood which He came down in His Son** *(Jesus Christ)* **to shed on the Cross for all humanity**. If you do not believe in Him and come to Him by His Son Jesus Christ, when you die, **you leave Him no choice but to judge you for your sins and send you to hell.** Moreover, you saw that **no man** or **man-made god** was able to prevent Him **from doing His will at Rapture** and they also are not be able to **prevent Him from sending anyone to hell.**

All Your Sacrifices have been to Devils

All your Hindu, Buddhist and pagan sacrifices have been to demons or devils and the <u>Almighty God is not pleased</u>

with your worship of devils. He created you higher and better than them. The devils that possess or enter into your graven images are deceptive spirits that are going to be destroyed by God and no human being is supposed to have anything to do with them—**1 Corinthians 10:20:**

> "But I say, that **the things which the Gentiles sacrifice, they sacrifice to devils, and not to God**: and **I would not that ye should have fellowship with devils.**"

The Gentiles are the non-Jewish nations of the world. Unfortunately, they all worship idols; aka devils. These idols are made of **Wood, Clay, Ceramic, Gold, Brass, Jade, other precious stones,** etc. Below is **how ridiculous the Almighty God thinks your worship of graven images or idols** is in **Isaiah 44:14-19:**

> "**He** *(the worshiper of graven idols)* **heweth him down cedars** *(cut down wood),* **and taketh the cypress and the oak, which he strengtheneth for himself among the trees of the forest**: he planteth an ash, and the rain doth nourish it. *15* **Then shall it be for a man to burn: for he will take thereof, and warm himself**; yea, he kindleth it, and baketh bread; yea, **he maketh a god, and worshippeth it; he maketh it a graven image, and falleth down thereto.**
>
> *16* He burneth part thereof in the fire; with part thereof he eateth flesh; he roasteth roast, and is satisfied: yea, he warmeth himself, and saith, Aha, I am warm, I have seen the fire: *17* **And the residue thereof he maketh a god, even his graven image: he falleth down unto it, and worshippeth it, and prayeth unto it, and saith, Deliver me; for thou art my god**.
>
> *18* They have not known nor understood: **for he** *(the devil)* **hath shut their eyes, that they cannot see; and their hearts, that they cannot understand.** *19* And none considereth in his heart,

> neither is there knowledge nor understanding <u>to say</u>, I have burned part of it in the fire; yea, also I have baked bread upon the coals thereof; I have roasted flesh, and eaten it: and shall I make the residue thereof an abomination? <u>shall I fall down to the stock of a tree?</u>"

Really think about it; how can you call an object *(idol)* that **you made or bought with your money a god**! I mean, **this is an object that you can smash to pieces if you want; how can it save you?** According to the scriptures above, the devil has deceived and blinded the eyes of all those who worship graven images that they cannot see or recognize how ridiculous their actions are.

I advise you to **read about why the Lord Jesus came into the world** because **you need to make Him your Lord if you ever hope to get into Heaven. For anyone that wants to come to the Lord Jesus and make Him his or her Lord and Savior,** I am repeating the **Prayer of Salvation** here because it is something you need to do before putting this book down. The information below will guide you on how to do it.

The Steps and Message of Salvation

To receive the Lord Jesus as your Savior, you must **believe the Good News** of the Word of God in **John 3:16-18:**

> **"For God so loved the world, that he gave his only begotten Son, that whosoever believeth in him should not perish, but have everlasting life**. For God sent not his Son into the world to condemn the world; but that the world through him might be saved. *18* **He that believeth on him is not condemned: but <u>he that believeth not is condemned already</u>,** because he hath not believed in the name of the only begotten Son of God."

You must also believe that the Lord Jesus is **the Only Way that you can get to God in Heaven** as stated in **Romans 10:9-10:**

> "That if thou shalt **confess with thy mouth the Lord Jesus, and shalt believe in thine heart that**

God hath raised him from the dead, thou shalt be saved. *10* For **with the heart man believeth unto righteousness; and with the mouth confession is made unto salvation."**

Pray the Prayer below **aloud** if you **believe** what is written in the Scriptures above:

The Prayer of Salvation

"Father, in the name of the Lord Jesus, I come to You because **I believe that Jesus Christ is Your Son and that He came into the world in the flesh. I believe that He was crucified on the Cross for my sins, died and was buried but on the third day, You raised Him from the dead**.

Lord Jesus, today, I renounce Hinduism, Buddhism and all other pagan practices that I was ever involved in. **I repent of all of them and I ask You to forgive me all my sins and wash me with Your blood from them all. I also repent of everything that I have done wrong from the day that I came out of mother's womb and forgive me for the idols that I worshiped in Hinduism, Buddhism and other pagan practices.** Please, come into my heart and be my Lord for I surrender to Your Lordship this day and forever. Give me Your eternal life for I declare that I belong to You from now on.

I also ask You to **give me Your Holy Spirit** to keep me in Your will, teach me the Bible, lead and protect me. I choose to do only those things that please You from now on. Father, I believe that You heard me and that I am now your child. Thank You for giving me Your Son and Your Holy Spirit. I receive them in the name of the Lord Jesus; Amen."

Chapter 18
Crucifixion was the Only Way to Kill Jesus

This section of the book will discuss the **significance of the Lord Jesus' Crucifixion on the Cross** and why the Cross **was the only way God ordained** for the Lord Jesus to die for our sins. **He could have been killed any other way but God chose the Cross for Him.** In this chapter we are going to see why.

The Method of Crucifixion?

The **Crucifixion** method of punishment by death was designed to inflict the **maximum effect of shame, public humiliation, agonizing pain and slow death by suffocation on the victim.** It is believed that the Assyrians and the Babylonians invented it and that Alexander the Great brought it to the Mediterranean. The **Romans adopted** and **used it** because it was the **most brutal and shameful** way of killing someone.

The Divine Design of the Cross

To the Lord Jesus' killers, the Cross was meant to bring **shame and public humiliation to Him** but from **God's perspective, the Cross speaks the 'Message of Redemption':**

1. **The vertical part of it, points to:**
   - God in Heaven and His mercy towards humanity
   - Earth and those who dwell on it
   - It was dropped in a hole on the ground for things under the earth—hell and the evil underworld forces that Jesus Christ's death defeated
2. **The horizontal part of it, points to:**
   - The sins that are past
   - The sins in the future as you repent when you commit them

Christ Carried Our Humiliations and Reproaches Away

God the Father chose that the Lord had to die by the 'death of the Cross' because, He intended to make **the Lord Jesus to become our sin.** Yes, **He wanted Him to trade places with us and become a public spectacle of shame, ridicule and an object of humiliation** along with all the reproaches that come upon a sinful person which is what we all deserved under His judgment. In other words, **God the Father made His Son Jesus Christ to go through all the punishment that would have come upon us sinners**.

To attest to **His divine plan** that **the Cross** would be the way for His Son *(Jesus Christ)* to die, God made sure that the **Lord's 'death on the Cross' was foretold 500 years before His birth**. Also, many of His prophets even gave specific details about how He will be treated, the nature of the wounds and the afflictions that He will suffer. Below is one of the Prophecies in **Isaiah 53:3-10** given 500 years before Christ was born:

> "**He** *(Jesus)* **is despised and rejected of men; a man of sorrows, and acquainted with grief: and we hid as it were our faces from him; he was despised, and we esteemed him not. 4 Surely he hath borne our griefs, and carried our sorrows: yet we did esteem him stricken, smitten of God, and afflicted** *(we erroneously thought that He was being punished by God for His own wrong doing)*.
>
> **5 But he was wounded for our transgressions, he was bruised for our iniquities: the chastisement of our peace was upon him; and with his stripes we are healed.** 6 All we like sheep have gone astray; we have turned everyone to his own way; **and the LORD hath laid on Him the iniquity of us all…**
>
> 9 And he made his grave with the wicked *(the thieves crucified with Him),* and with the rich in his death *(a rich man buries Him in his own grave);* **because he had done no violence, neither was any deceit in his mouth** *(He was faultless).* 10 **Yet it pleased the LORD to bruise him; he hath put him to grief: <u>when thou shalt make his Soul an Offering for sin,</u> he shall see His Seed** *(those who believe in Him),* he *(believers tell others about Him)* shall prolong his days, and the pleasure of the LORD shall prosper in his hand."

I want you to know that, the **Cross was not yet invented** when these specific details of the manner of Christ's death were written in **Psalm 22:6-18:**

> "But I *(Jesus)* **am a worm, and no man; a reproach of men, and despised of the people.** *7* **All they that see me laugh me to scorn: they shoot out the lip, they shake the head,** saying, *8* **He trusted on the LORD that he would deliver him: let him deliver him, seeing he delighted in him.**
>
> *14* **I am poured out like water, and all my bones are out of joint: my heart is like wax; it is melted in the midst of my bowels.** *15* My strength is dried up like a potsherd; and my tongue cleaveth to my jaws; and **thou** *(God)* **hast brought me into the Dust of Death.** *16* For dogs have compassed me: the assembly of the wicked have inclosed me: **they pierced my hands and my feet** *(the nails of the Cross)*. *17* I may tell all my bones: **they look and stare upon me.** *18* **They part my garments among them, and cast lots upon my vesture."**

The prophecies were fulfilled in Christ as foretold while He was on the Cross. Also, in **Isaiah 52:13-15**, we are **told that Christ's face and body will be disfigured more than any other human being.** We know that as a result of **all the marks on His body from severe beatings, carrying the sicknesses and diseases of every human being that ever lived on earth and will ever live, He was very <u>badly disfigured</u>:**

> "Behold, my servant shall deal prudently, he shall be exalted and extolled, and be very high. *14* As many were astonied at thee; **His Visage** *(entire body)* **was so marred more than any man, and his form more than the sons of men**: *15* **So shall he sprinkle many nations** *(God will use His blood to sprinkle us clean from our sins)*; the kings shall shut their mouths at him *(while hanging on the Cross, they mocked Him)*: **for that which had not been told**

them shall they see *(it was a strange sight for God's Son to be battered and die shamefully)*; and that which they had not heard shall they consider."

To attest to the **accuracy and the infallibility of God's Word,** all the prophecies spoken by God 500 years before His birth in Isaiah 52:13-15, all of Isaiah 53 and Psalm 22:6-18 were literally suffered by Christ on the way to the Cross and while <u>on the Cross for our sins</u>.

The Lord Jesus became Our Sin on the Cross

That the <u>sinner becomes</u> **rejected by God** is revealed to us in scripture way back in the days of Moses when the children of Israel were murmuring against God in the wilderness. For this sin, many of them were **bitten by fiery serpents and began to die.** As a result, Moses cried out to the Lord in **Numbers 21:8-9**:

"And the LORD said unto Moses, Make thee **a fiery serpent, and set it upon a pole** *(a type of Cross)*: and **it shall come to pass, that every one that is bitten, <u>when he looketh upon it</u>, shall live.**

9 And Moses made a serpent of brass, and put it upon a pole *(cross)*, and it came to pass, that if **a Serpent** *(symbol of sin)* **had bitten any man, <u>when he beheld the serpent of brass</u>** *(a type of Christ on the Cross)*, **he lived."**

The '**brass serpent**' represented the **sin** of the children of Israel and when <u>Christ was on the Cross</u>, **He too became the sin of every human being!** We can safely say that in the beginning, Adam and Eve were bitten by the serpent along with the rest of humanity and <u>Christ is the antidote</u>. Therefore, the **Lord Jesus needed to carry away on His Cross, all the sins of both the Jews and the Gentiles** in His death and He did. Just as in the days of Moses, <u>**anyone who now looks up to Him**</u>, is **saved from his or her sins.**

This is why we were told in **2 Corinthians 5:21** that the Lord Jesus was **made sin for us.** While on the Cross, **Jesus Christ <u>became our very sin;</u>** God turned Him into our sin so that <u>He **can punish our sins in Him**</u>. This is because only Jesus Christ can withstand God's severe blows of punishment on sin:

"For **he hath made him to be sin for us, who knew no sin**; that we might be made the righteousness of God in him."

Remember God's Word in **Ezekiel 18:4** which says, "**The soul that sins shall die**;' meaning that **God has a 'death penalty' on sin**. As a result, we all deserved God's death penalty for our sins which means **eternal separation from God in hell.** Instead of **damning us all** to hell, <u>God in His mercy sent His Son Jesus Christ</u> to **take away His judgment on us sinners**; meaning **every human being.**

Christ Became Accursed on the Cross for Us

Another reason that Christ had to die on the Cross was so that **He can take all our curses upon Himself** for both Jews and Gentiles. Sin brings a curse on the sinner and since every human being has many sins, we all were under many curses from God. As a result, the world is **not only full of <u>sins</u> but of <u>curses</u>** because **every act of sin makes a person become 'accursed' or cursed by God**. The divine plan of God was to make the Lord Jesus become an 'Accursed Person' with our sin!

<u>**The Lord Jesus knew that He was going to be lifted up on the Cross as an accursed for our sin and that He will then draw us all to Him**</u> as He said in **John 12:32-33:**

"And <u>**I, if I be lifted up from the earth**</u>, will draw all men unto me. 33 This he said, <u>signifying what death he should die</u> *(on the Cross)*."

Again, every sin carries a curse, Christ's 'form of death' had to be the type that will **pay for each specific curse that was upon us**. Therefore, the **Cross which will make Him accursed was <u>the most appropriate way for Him to carry our curses away</u>**. This is why **God the Father chose hanging on a Tree** *(the Cross)* as His manner of death. We see **that anyone that is <u>hanged on a tree is cursed</u>** by God in **Deuteronomy 21:22-23:**

"And if a man have **committed a sin worthy of death**, and he be to be put to death, and **Thou Hang Him on a Tree:** 23 His body shall not remain all night upon the tree, but thou shalt in any wise bury him that day; **(for He that is Hanged is Accursed of God)**; that thy land be not defiled, which the LORD thy God giveth thee for an inheritance."

The Lord Jesus needed to carry our sins and curses out of the earth to the realm of the dead so that we can be free of them. This is why He literally became accursed or cursed by God for our sakes as we learn in **Galatians 3:13**:

"**Christ hath redeemed us from the curse** of the law *(all human sins)*, **Being Made a Curse for Us**: for it is written, **Cursed is Every One that Hangeth on a Tree**."

You can now understand from the scriptures above that it was necessary for the Lord Jesus to be hung on the Cross and become accursed by God in order to receive God's Perfect Judgment on Sins and Curses on His Person for all humanity; **He had to die the 'death of a Sinner' for us all**! If He had not done it, God would have condemned all humanity to hell forever.

To God's glory, **His very obedient Lamb was glad to bear our sins, reproaches, shame**, etc., and to go to the Cross for us all as we see in in **Isaiah 50:6-7**:

"**I gave my back to the smiters, and my cheeks to them that plucked off the hair**: I hid not my face from shame and **spitting**. 7 For the Lord GOD will help me; therefore **shall I not be confounded**: therefore have I **set my face like a flint**, and I **know that I shall not be ashamed**."

As you can see above, this is the greatest love anyone can show to another or that a parent can show for his or her child. As a parent, even after Rapture, God made sure that whoever put their trust and faith in the Lord Jesus will be saved. God is the same yesterday, today and forever; He never changes. He still wants to save you if you let Him; so let Him.

Christ as the Accursed Scapegoat

God the Father held Jesus Christ responsible for all our sins and He was **God's Scapegoat** that was led outside the city wall of Jerusalem carrying the sins of the world upon Himself as required by God in **Leviticus 16:21-22**:

> "And Aaron shall lay both his hands upon the head of the live goat, and **confess over him all the iniquities of the children of Israel, and all their transgressions in all their sins, putting them upon the head of the goat,** and shall send him away by the hand of a fit man into the wilderness: 22 And **the goat shall bear upon him all their iniquities** unto **a land not inhabited:** and he shall let go the goat in the wilderness."

As you saw in the scriptures, Christ as the sin offering essentially became the scapegoat bearing all our sins into the land of the dead on His Cross *(into the wilderness)*. Christ became accursed with our sins and had to die outside the city taking our punishment away with Him.

Why God Separated Himself from Christ on the Cross

In **Hebrews 10:4-7**, we see that **God prepared a human body for His Word** *(Christ)* **and sent Him into the world for the purpose of sacrificing Him on the Cross as a Lamb** *(scapegoat)* **for our sins and curses.** The Lord Jesus was glad to do His Father's will which meant going to the Cross for us:

> "For it is not possible that the blood of bulls and of goats should take away sins *(only the blood of Christ takes away sin).* 5 Wherefore when he *(Jesus)* cometh into the world, he saith, Sacrifice and offering thou wouldest not, **but a body** *(a human body)* **hast thou prepared me**: 6 In burnt offerings and sacrifices for sin thou hast had no pleasure. 7 Then said I, Lo, I come (in the volume of the book it is written of me *{the Bible},)* **to do thy will, O God.**"

As you just read, it was necessary for **God to give His Word a human body;** *(the last Adam)* that **He can distance Himself from** in order to fully punish Him as the scapegoat for our **sins.** Therefore, as the Lord Jesus became accursed on the Cross in God's sight with our curses, God separated Himself from Him; His own Word. This is the only time in existence that **God separated Himself from the Word** *(Jesus)* **that came out of His mouth**.

God the Father needed to separate Himself from the Lord Jesus so that **Christ can be a 'regular man' that God holds accountable for the sin of the world**. This is why Jesus had to be on the Cross by Himself and why He cried out in **Psalm 22:1-21** as follows:

> "**My God, my God, why hast thou forsaken me?** **why art thou so far from helping me, and from the words of my roaring?**... *10* I was cast upon thee from the womb: thou art my God from my mother's belly. *11* Be not far from me; for trouble is near; for there is none to help... *19* **But be not thou far from me, O Lord: O my strength, haste thee to help me.** *20* Deliver my soul from the sword *(Roman soldiers)*; my darling from the power of the dog *(the devil)*. *21* Save me from the lion's mouth: for thou hast heard me from the horns of the unicorns."

Remember that Adam brought sin upon humanity by his disobedience. **The Lord Jesus had to became a regular man (last Adam) to be held responsible for our sins and curses so that God can pour out His full judgment and punishment on Him as our scapegoat!** Therefore, as a regular man, He obeyed God's commandment to go to the Cross, die, defeat death, defeat the devil and take the Authority over the Earth away from the devil — **Romans 5:18-19:**

> "Therefore as by the offence of one *(Adam)*, Judgment came Upon All Men to Condemnation; even so by the Righteousness of One *(the Lord Jesus)*, the free gift came Upon All Men unto Justification of Life *(being made right with God)*. *19* **For as by one man's disobedience many were made sinners, so by the obedience of one shall many be made righteous.**"

Truly, God punished sin in Christ for us while He was on the Cross; Christ paid for it all. This is why He is the only way to escape the devil and be reconciled with God.

The Cross Shows How Man is Clueless about God's Ways

No one knew what God was doing with Christ on the Cross; actually, the people would not have believed that God's will was at work in Him on the Cross. As foretold, while Christ was on the Cross, the people passing by, the Scribes, the Elders and the Chief Priests, **all Mocked Him** as they watched **Him in agony, suffocating and slowly dying on the Cross because, they knew very well** <u>what</u> the 'Death of the Cross' <u>meant for anyone</u>— an '<u>accursed</u>' by God! We see this in **Matthew 27:29-43:**

> "And when **they had platted a crown of thorns, they put it upon his head, and a reed in his right hand: and they bowed the knee before him, and** <u>mocked him</u>, saying, Hail, King of the Jews! 30 And **they spit upon him**, and took the reed, and **smote him on the head.** 31 And after that they had mocked him, they took the robe off from him, and put his own raiment on him, and led him away <u>to crucify him</u>…
> 35 And they crucified him, and parted his garments, casting lots: that it might be fulfilled which was spoken by the prophet, They parted my garments among them, and upon my vesture did they cast lots…39 And they that **passed by reviled him, wagging their heads,** 40 And saying, **Thou that destroyest the temple, and buildest it in three days, save thyself.** <u>If thou be the Son of God</u>, come down from the cross.
> 41 Likewise also **the chief priests mocking him,** with the scribes and elders, said, 42 **He saved others; himself he cannot save.** If he be the King of Israel, let him now come down from the cross, and we will believe him. 43 **He trusted in God; let him deliver him now, if he** *(God)* **will have him: for he said, I am the Son of God.**"

The people and their leaders were so sure that God had nothing to do with Christ because of the manner of His death. **There-**

fore, the leaders taught that they had successfully silenced Him by killing Him in a shameful and humiliating way.

Christ Satisfied God's Wrath on Sin and the Sinner

As you have seen above, **God did not spare His son from receiving the full punishment that we sinners rightly deserved.** No one who was witnessing Christ's death on the Cross **had any clue as to what God was doing. They had no idea that God's full wrath was being poured out on Christ as He became our sin and that God was using His death to pay for our sins. The Lord Jesus <u>satisfied God's anger or wrath</u> against sin and the sinner for us all.** He received all the punishment that God required from every human soul that sinned!

God Almighty had to take this very drastic action of sacrificing His own Son on the Cross because sin is an 'Eternal Seed of Corruption and Decay;' a stain that nothing can remove but God's own Blood. This is why He came down in His Word *(Jesus)* and shed it on the Cross for us.

The Lord Jesus Commanded His Own Death on the Cross

The Lord told us in **John 10:17-18** that **no man can take His Life from Him** but that He will lay it down of His own will; <u>no man can kill Him</u>:

> "Therefore doth my Father love me, because **I lay down my life, that I might take it again.** *18* **No man taketh it from me, but I lay it down of myself. I have power to lay it down, and I have power to take it again.** This commandment have I received of my Father."

Know that God is no respecter of persons; what He says to one He says to all including Christ when He was here as a man as we see in the following scripture. As long **as the Lord Jesus' feet were touching the ground, He could not be killed** because He exercises <u>dominion</u> everywhere He stands — **Joshua 1:3-5:**

> "**<u>Every place that the sole of your foot shall tread upon, that have I given unto you</u>,** as I said unto Moses... *5* **There shall not any man be able to stand before thee all the days of thy life: as I**

was with Moses, so I will be with thee: I will not fail thee, nor forsake thee."

Also, every ground the feet of the Lord Jesus touches becomes holy as we saw when Moses (**Exodus 3:5**) and Joshua (**Joshua 5:15**) stood before Him. This is the reason you see the Lord Jesus barefoot in visions because His feet sanctify the ground they touch. Even while on the Cross, they could still not kill Him. Therefore, before the Lord Jesus could die, **He released His own spirit and sent it to God**; meaning that **He was in command of His own death** as written in **Luke 23:46:**

> "And when Jesus had cried with a loud voice, he said, **Father, into thy hands I commend my spirit**: and having said thus, **he gave up the ghost.**"

What Christ Did in Hell

After the Lord died on the Cross, He descended into hell and this is recorded in **Colossians 2:15** about what He did there:

> "And **having spoiled principalities and powers, he made a shew of them openly, triumphing over them** in it."

The Lord **victoriously avenged** all humanity by tramping **the devil and his forces in an open disgrace for the spirit world to see!** As He made me to understand, **He stepped on the devil's head, yanked out his tongue** with which he had **blasphemed** and **reproached God** and **took away** the *(Key)* **'Adamic Authority'** over the earth from him. When the Lord showed me a vision of the way the devil really looks now, I saw a huge dent on his head and he cannot speak.

This is why the devil fights people with thoughts and uses people to speak negative words over others. Before His death, the Lord was so sure that **He would take back the 'Adamic Authority' over the earth** from the devil that He gave it to us even before He was crucified as we see in **Luke 10:19:**

> "Behold, **I give unto you power** *(authority over the earth)* **to tread on serpents and scorpions, and over**

all the power of the enemy *(the devil and his forces)*: and nothing shall by any means hurt you."

Also in **Luke 9:1**:

"Then he called his twelve disciples together, and **gave them power and authority over all devils,** and to cure diseases."

Christ Displayed the Greatest Strength on Earth

The Cross of Jesus Christ demonstrated the **greatest strength ever displayed on earth.** To understand this, think about all the dead people *(billions of them)* that have lived on earth and the 8 billion that were on earth before Rapture. The Lord Jesus **carried on His body,** all the sins and afflictions of humanity such as sicknesses and diseases, plagues, curses and all the evil deeds that resulted in every human suffering.

Think of the mental afflictions alone; afflictions such as madness, insomnia, migraine, schizophrenia, epilepsy, demon possession, etc., that plagued about 30 billion people *(a conservative estimate of the human population of all time),* **placed on One Man—the Lord Jesus.** For example, the 'Demoniac' possessed by 'Legion' that the Lord Jesus encountered in **Mark 5:9, had in him alone 3,000 to 6,000** *(legion)* **demons!**

Also, think about all the skin diseases that cause lesions on the skin, diseases such as Syphilis, Aids, ancient plagues, etc., laid on the same Man; Jesus. From what God the Father showed me in a vision, the **weight of all the human sins, sicknesses and diseases, afflictions, beatings from the forces of the High Priest, the Roman soldiers and from the 'Scourging Post,'** all contributed to make Christ **delirious and weak as He staggered** on His way to the Cross.

At the same time, **His enemies spat, mocked, jeered and threw rocks at Him** without knowing that **He was the Lamb of God** that was **born to be sacrificed for their sin and the sin of humanity.** Can you imagine one human being taking upon Himself all the diseases in the world and not to talk about our sins and their heavy weight? **The Lord Jesus was the only man in Heaven and on earth that could carry the weight of the sins of the world and He did it among the most hostile people.**

In addition to all this, all the demons in hell and the devil at their helm were on hand to inspire the people to demand His crucifixion, to do the most wicked things to Him, and to **make Him die the most agonizing slow and painful death on record.** To make matters worse for the Lord Jesus, God the Father who cannot look upon sin, had to separate Himself from His Son; His Word for the first time since His existence! **The Lord Jesus had to accomplish the 'Works of the Cross'** as a 'Regular Man.' Again, the reason for this was because God gave Adam *(man)* the Authority over the earth and he ignorantly gave it away to the devil in his willful sin.

God Way's and Wisdom at the Cross of Jesus Christ

Again, no one among the people at **Jesus' execution discerned that the Wisdom of God was at work in Him for all of us sinners!** It confirmed what God told us in **Isaiah 55:8-9** that **His ways and thoughts are different from our ways and thoughts**. He demonstrated the vast differences between His ways and our ways by what He did in His Son; both on the way to the Cross and on the Cross.

As a result of the differences between His ways and our ways, not one person thought that God was anywhere to be found while the Lord Jesus was being crucified:

> **"For <u>my thoughts are not your thoughts</u>, neither are <u>your ways my ways</u>, saith the LORD. 9 For as the heavens are higher than the earth, so are my ways higher than your ways, and my thoughts than your thoughts."**

Another clear difference between God's ways and man's ways is revealed in the definition of 'human strength.'

How God Views Human Strength

An example of the differences between man's ways and God's ways is also seen in how man views '**Human Strength**' and how God sees it. Man defines human strength as the "quality of being physically strong" *(power and might),* while **<u>God defines human strength</u>** as the Lord Jesus informed us in **2 Corinthians 12:9**:

"And he said unto me, My grace is sufficient for thee: **for <u>my strength is made perfect in weakness</u>.** Most gladly therefore will I rather glory in my infirmities *(weaknesses)*, that the power of Christ may rest upon me."

He told us that '**Human Strength**' is '**Made Perfect**' in <u>**Weakness**</u> and He demonstrated it by His Cross. **It was astounding to see in a vision the Lord Jesus staggering and extremely delirious with no strength but determined to keep moving on His way to the Cross.** From what God did for us all with Christ on the Cross, we can see that strength is not just power and might. We also see God's ways and Wisdom by what He did when He raised Christ from the dead; He again, demonstrated the greatness of His power — **Ephesians 1:19-23:**

"And what is the <u>**exceeding greatness of his power**</u> to us-ward who believe, according to the working of his mighty power, 20 **Which he wrought in Christ, when he raised him from the dead, and set him at his own right hand in the heavenly places,**

21 <u>**Far above all principality, and power, and might, and dominion, and every name that is named,**</u> **not only in this world, but also in that which is to come:** 22 And hath <u>**put all things under his feet**</u>, and <u>**gave him to be the head over all things**</u> to the church, 23 Which is his body, the fulness of him that filleth all in all."

You can now see why the Apostle Paul exclaimed in the following words in **Romans 11:33:**

"O the depth of the riches both of the <u>**wisdom and knowledge of God**</u>! how unsearchable are his judgments, and his ways past finding out!"

Christ and His Cross is the Only Way to Escape the Devil

As we have seen in a previous chapter, ever since **Adam yielded his authority to the devil, sin has dominated humanity** and **sin has the propensity to grow** and branch out into other various forms of evil in those who rebel against the Word of God. It is one of the reasons that **people get**

deeper and deeper into other forms of criminal and ungodly behaviors when they choose not to live by the Word of God that is written in the Bible — **Romans 6:16-18:**

> "**Know ye not, that to whom ye yield yourselves servants to obey, his servants ye are to whom ye obey**; whether of sin unto death, or of obedience unto righteousness? *17* But God be thanked, **that ye were the servants of sin**, but ye have obeyed from the heart that form of doctrine which was delivered you. *18* **Being then made free from sin, ye became the servants of righteousness.**"

God gives every human being that comes into His earth, the opportunity to **choose good over evil**; He wants us to have a **'free will'** but **to use it for good. Even the Lord Jesus was not exempted from this** but rather, **He was delivered up to the devil to be tempted with evil but He did not sin** as Adam did. It takes the **'Finished Works of Christ'** on the Cross to **set anyone who is willing, free from the bondage of sin.**

Ever since the Lord Jesus paid the full price for our sins on the Cross, anyone who does not want to use their free will for evil but for good can run to Him. **Christ is the only way to escape the devil's bondage**; anyone who wills, can come out of it by Christ. You cannot choose to do good without belonging to Christ and all those who receive Christ will be saved; they are **no longer slaves to sin.**

On the other hand, **all those who reject Him, do not belong to or receive Him as their Lord are still under the direct control of the devil who continues to use sin to hold them as his slaves.** This is because by rejecting Christ or refusing to come to Him, they remain under the **'Adamic Covenant' with the devil; meaning that they still belong to the devil. Rejecting Christ means rejecting God and Heaven.**

Summary of Christ's Payment for Our Sins

Note the different punishments for our sins which the Lord Jesus received through the shameful, agonizing, prolonged suffering and death on the Cross. I want you to note that for **every single thing that He suffered, He was paying for one of our specific sins** as you see below:

1. His Wounds were for our transgression; disobeying God's Commandments
2. His Bruises were for our iniquities; choosing to do things our way, instead of God's
3. The Bible tells us in **Proverbs 19:29** that His stripes were for our foolishness:

    "Judgments are prepared for scorners, and **stripes for the back of fools**."

    And in **Proverbs 26:3**, it says:

    "A whip for the horse, a bridle for the ass, and **a rod for the fool's back**."

4. He took on Himself, all our **sicknesses and diseases and they marred or disfigured Him** more than any other human being; past or present— **Isaiah 52:14:**

    "As many were astonied at thee; his visage (Jesus' looks on the Cross) was so marred *(disfigured)* **more than any man, and his form more than the sons of men** *(any human being)*."

5. They **pierced** His hands and feet to fulfill God's judgment on the <u>seed of the woman</u> by the serpent *(devil)* in **Genesis 3:15:**

    "**And I will put enmity between thee** *(the devil)* **and the woman** *(Eve and all her descendants),* **and between thy Seed** *(those who yield themselves to the devil)* **and Her Seed** *(fulfilled in Jesus);* <u>**it shall bruise thy head**</u> *(when He died, the Lord Jesus descended into hell and Stomped on the devil's head),* and <u>**thou shalt bruise his heel**</u> *(those instigated by the devil <u>pierced Jesus' feet with nails</u>).*"

6. The **stripes He received were for our healing;** "by His stripes we are healed."
7. His **agony and torment were for our peace**
8. His **death satisfied God's 'death penalty'** for us all

Chapter 19
The Power of God's Love and Forgiveness

Throughout this book, you have read about how **God loves us and that He Himself came down to earth in His Word; Jesus to save us from our sins.** I want you to know that **nothing holds a candle to or can be compared** to the **awesome power of the love and forgiveness that is only found in Christianity** and nowhere else!

Also, there are **no belief systems, religions or forms of worship** that can be compared to the love and forgiveness that God gave us through His Son Jesus Christ. God told me that **forgiveness is, "Letting people off the hook".** It means looking past people's faults and letting go of the wrong they did to you. They may never tell you that they are sorry for what they did to you but you choose to forgive them because God forgave you all your sins against Him.

To man, love is a feeling but not with God. The reason for this is because biblically, **Love is a Person**; the Person of God Himself! This is why the Bible tells us in **1 John 4:7-8** that **God is Love**:

> "Beloved, **let us love one another: for love is of God; and every one that loveth is born of God, and knoweth God.** *8* He that loveth not knoweth not God; for **God is love.**"

Only the love that God gives us can <u>make us care for others</u>. No one can truly love without first receiving God into his or her life through Christ. **God's 'Agape' love is different; it is an unconditional love.** It is not based on anything else but the desire to care, nurture and protect no matter what. This is the true love that **cares about other people hoping for nothing in return.**

Because the world thinks that <u>love is a feeling</u>, many people 'fall-in and out-of- love' on a regular basis. What they do not realize is that their feelings are the results of **lust,**

selfishness or self-seeking and the pride of showing off for others to see. Therefore, many men base their love on the beautiful looks of a woman and many women also love a man for his looks, status, money or material possessions. When these things go away or fade, so does the love these people professed.

Your Turn to Show People Love and Forgiveness

When you become a Christian, you learn that love and forgiveness are the root of Christianity. You also learn that, **God so loved us that <u>He chose to forgive us our sin against Him</u> rather than destroy us. It is now your turn to both forgive and love those around you even as you are now living in the most depraved time after Rapture.** As a result of what God did by forgiving us our sins, He expects us to love and forgive others as well.

When Adam and Eve sinned against Him, He immediately sprang into action by **killing an innocent Lamb *(Jesus)* and covering them with its blood and skin — Genesis 3:9-21:**

> "And the LORD God called unto Adam, and said unto him, Where art thou? *10* And he said, I heard thy voice in the garden, and I was afraid, because I was naked; and I hid myself. *11* And he said, Who told thee that thou wast naked?
>
> Hast thou eaten of the tree, whereof I commanded thee that thou shouldest not eat? *12* And the man said, The woman whom thou gavest to be with me, she gave me of the tree, and I did eat... *(after judging them), 21* **Unto Adam also and to his wife did the LORD God make coats of skins, and clothed them."**

God loved and forgave us way back in Adam and at the appropriate time, He manifested this Love and Forgiveness by sending His only begotten Son to the Cross for our sins. While dying on the Cross, the Lord Jesus forgave and asked

God the Father to forgive those who were killing Him as we see in **Luke 23:34:**

> "Then said Jesus, **Father, forgive them; for they know not what they do.**"

Now it is your turn to love and forgive.

All Tribulation Saints Must Love and Forgive

As a Tribulation Saint, love and forgiveness will help you survive the days you are now in. **No matter what happens, you must love and forgive even those who want to kill you or who betray you.** This is because the entire Christian faith is based solely on God's love and forgiveness that humanity **did not deserve but was freely given to us by God in His Mercy.**

You will notice in the scripture below that when Adam and Eve sinned and God confronted them, **rather than repenting and asking for His mercy, they played the 'Blame Game.'** Eve blamed the serpent and Adam blamed both God and Eve — **Genesis 3:11-13:**

> "And he said, Who told thee that thou wast naked? Hast thou eaten of the tree, whereof I commanded thee that thou shouldest not eat? 12 And the man said, **The woman whom thou gavest to be with me, she gave me** of the tree, and I did eat. 13 And the LORD God said unto the woman, What is this that thou hast done? And the woman said, **The serpent beguiled me,** and I did eat."

In spite of their unrepentant hearts, God in His mercy saved them for His own sake — **this is love.** They did not deserve God's forgiveness and neither do we. **Every one of us is as guilty as Adam and Eve were because we have all disobeyed God's Word in one form or another.** It is why **Romans 5:6-10** says:

> "**For when we were yet without strength, in due time Christ died for the ungodly.** 7 For scarcely for a righteous man will one die: yet peradventure for a good man some would even dare to die. 8

> **But God commendeth his love toward us**, in that, **while we were yet sinners**, Christ died for us.
>
> 9 Much more then, **being now justified by his blood, we shall be saved from wrath through him.** 10 For **if, when we were enemies, we were reconciled to God by the death of his Son, much more, being reconciled, we shall be saved by his life.**"

As you can see above, God forgave and reconciled us to Himself in Christ not because we deserved it but because He loves us. Therefore, do not wait for people to deserve your forgiveness before you choose to forgive them. As a matter of fact, the Lord Jesus told us that, if we do not forgive others, our Heavenly Father will also not forgive us our sins — **Matthew 6:14-15:**

> **"For if ye forgive men their trespasses, your heavenly Father will also forgive you:** 15 **But if ye forgive not men their trespasses, neither will your Father forgive your trespasses.**"

We again read about it in the Lord's parable of the wicked servant in **Matthew 18:23-35.** The Lord Jesus repeated that a **Christian who does not forgive others will not be forgiven by God the Father either**:

> "Therefore is the kingdom of heaven likened unto a certain king, which would take account of his servants. 24 And when he had begun to reckon, one was brought unto him, **which owed him ten thousand talents**. 25 But forasmuch as he had not to pay, his lord commanded him to be sold, and his wife, and children, and all that he had, and payment to be made.
>
> 26 The servant therefore fell down, and worshipped him, saying, Lord, have patience with me, and I will pay thee all. 27 **Then the lord of that servant was moved with compassion, and loosed him, and forgave him the debt.** 28 But the same servant went out, and found one of his fellowservants,

which owed him an hund-red pence: and he laid hands on him, and took him by the throat, saying, Pay me that thou owest.

29 **And his fellowservant fell down at his feet, and besought him, saying, Have patience with me, and I will pay thee all.** *30* **And he would not: but went and cast him into prison, till he should pay the debt.** *31* So when his fellowservants saw what was done, they were very sorry, and came and told unto their lord all that was done. *32* Then his lord, after that he had called him, said unto him, **O thou wicked servant, I forgave thee all that debt, because thou desiredst me:**

33 Shouldest not thou also have had compassion on thy fellowservant, even as I had pity on thee? *34* And his lord was wroth, and delivered him to the tormentors, till he should pay all that was due unto him. *35* **So likewise shall my heavenly Father do also unto you, if ye from your hearts forgive not everyone his brother their trespasses."**

The Non-Christian Perspective on Forgiveness

Speaking as one who once practiced Islam, my initial reaction to the **Christian practice of forgiveness** was shocking. When you are not a Christian and a Christian says to you, **"I forgive you,"** it makes you <u>**do a double take in shock.**</u> Many people from other religions also have this reaction. This was my experience to forgiveness because of my previous Islamic belief in revenge.

For example, before being Born Again, you cannot imagine my reaction to a colleague who told me that **she went to visit her late daughter's boyfriend who was serving time in prison for killing her!** She also told me that she forgave him and prays for him. I truly thought there was something wrong with her.

Today, you can still see **those who share the Islamic radical beliefs blowing up themselves and many others that they consider to be their enemies**. This is because there is **no love or forgiveness in their belief system**. In fact, their beliefs and practices are the **opposite of love and forgiveness — revenge and retaliation!**

It is why when you are a non-Christian from this religion, you genuinely believe that there is something wrong with those who forgive and 'let people get one over on them.' As a non-Christian, when you continue to interact with Christians, you begin to notice that **not only do they mean it when they forgive; it is actually a way of life for them.** It was only when I became Born Again and received the Baptism of the Holy Spirit that I began to understand love and forgiveness from God's perspective.

Therefore, as a Tribulation Saint, you need to shine your Light — the life of Christ in you on those still in darkness around you. The greater the darkness in the world, the brighter His light in you should shine. Therefore, love and forgive others; teach it to those around you.

Chapter 20
Why the Souls in Hell Cannot Die

Definition of Hell

Hell is defined as a spiritual realm of evil spirits and of suffering. It is a place beneath the earth where the wicked are punished with perpetual fire. Simply put, it is a horrible place that everyone in their right mind should avoid at all cost by running to Christ.

God Created Hell for the Devil and the Fallen Angels

The Lord Jesus told us in **Matthew 25:41** that, <u>God never created hell for man</u> but for the devil and his fallen angels:

> "Then shall he *(Jesus)* say also unto them on the left hand, Depart from me, ye cursed, into **everlasting fire, prepared for the devil and his angels.**"

God designed hell as a place to **mete out His maximum punishment on the devil and the fallen angels for their rebellion against Him and for their wickedness against humanity.** God never designed hell for the human soul because the conditions there are unbearable. The question is: **How did man end up as a candidate for hell?**

How Man Become a Candidate for Hell

The answer to the question is that **man's rebellion against God's Word made him a candidate for hell. When <u>man rejected God, he by default</u>, chose a union with the devil and his wicked evil ways.** Adam and Eve chose **the devil's lies over God's Word which is the <u>only Truth in the universe</u>.** We saw in **Romans 5:12** that, Adam passed this rebellion to all humanity:

> "Wherefore, as **by one man sin entered into the world, and death by sin**; and so **death passed upon all men,** for **that all have sinned**..."

As soon as Adam was in union with the devil, the devil wasted no time but quickly began to teach Adam and his descendants his evil and wicked ways. **This is why you do not have to teach a child how to lie, it comes naturally to them from the devil!** Before Christ, we were all under the devil's bondage to sin so, those who rejected Christ by default chose to remain under the devil.

As a result, in societies today, through a life of sin, many people **have turned their lives totally over to the devil** and we are told that **all who commit sin** *(walk contrary to the Word of God in the Bible)*, **belong to the devil** — **1 John 3:8**:

> "**He that committeth sin is of the devil;** for the devil sinneth from the beginning."

God regards all 'unrepentant sinners' **after hearing the Gospel and all those who rejected His Word as children of the devil**. The Lord Jesus showed us this in **John 8:44**:

> "**Ye are of your father the devil, and the lusts of your father ye will do.** He was a murderer from the beginning, and abode not in the truth, **because there is no truth in him**. When he speaketh a lie, he speaketh of his own: **for he is a liar, and the father of it**."

The devil lied to Eve; through her and Adam brought death on humanity. You can see the devastation of this each time you attend a funeral. Many people follow the devils' evil ways and the Lord calls them children of the devil. Therefore, you are a child of the devil if you:
1. Murder
2. Lie
3. Steal
4. Cheat
5. Fornicate
6. Money or materialism is your god
7. Commit iniquity — doing your own will
8. Worship other gods — idols (paganism)
9. Blaspheme God's name
10. Mock God's ways or Word

11. Commit adultery or fornication
12. Practice homosexuality, transgender and other sexual perversions
13. Live for pleasure, power, fame and prominent positions instead of godliness

As you can see from scriptures, **all sin makes one a child of the devil** and a **candidate to join him in hell.** As a result, God had to send the 'unrepentant men and women' to hell to have the devil lord it over them there *(Adam's choice in the Garden).* At the end, they and the devil will be **thrown into the Lake of Fire.**

Those in an 'Eternal State of Decay' are only Fit for Hell

God has to **destroy all who carry in their soul and bodies, the 'Eternal Seed of Corruption and Decay' of sin** because again, nothing can remove their stain but God's own blood which they rejected when they were alive on earth. In other words, **God came down in His Word** *(Jesus)* **to shed His blood on the Cross for us all and all those who did not allow God to wash away the stain, decay, corruption and stench of sin from them** are sent to hell.

They are **forever contaminated and defiled in God's sight;** they are in an eternal state of decay that stinks but they cannot die. Again, **they did not accept the Lord Jesus' payment for their sins on the Cross** so, **God has to send them to hell where the devil whom they chose and his demons do to them what they did to others on earth as payment for their sins.** They will later be **thrown into the Lake of Fire** because nothing more can be done for them and God cannot look at them. From what you have read so far, you can now see or conclude that God does not send people to hell but He gives everyone their choice *(hell)* when they reject Christ.

Why Hell is the Way It Is

Hell is the way it is because **God and His Presence are not there.** It is a place for those:

• Who **wanted nothing to do with God;** cast His word behind their backs

- Who **had no time for God** due to their pursuit of wealth, fame, prestige
- Who **sold their souls to the devil to do evil** or for money and fame
- Who **did not believe that God existed**; became their own gods
- Who **worshipped idols** or other gods
- **Refused to accept God's gift of Salvation** in Jesus Christ
- Received the message of Salvation but **refused to change their evil ways**

Because hell is **lacking the Person and Presence of God**, it has **none of the attributes of the goodness of God** that people enjoy on earth. Therefore, in hell, there is:

- No **eternal life** with God
- No **fresh air**
- No **love**, compassion or caring
- No **mercy**
- No **light**, sun, moon or stars
- No **forgiveness**
- No **freedom**
- No **peace** or rest
- No **sleep** forever
- No **grace**; a second chance, or do-over
- No **beauty** but ugly and terrifying demons
- No **food** but there is hunger
- No **flavor**, scent, fragrance or good smell
- No **water** or anything to quench your thirst
- No **plants**, greenery or cool breeze
- No **kindness**
- No **goodness**
- No **good health**
- No **joy,** smile or laughter
- No **relief** from pain and torment
- No **refreshment**
- No **death**
- No **exit**

While on earth, **people take all these things which are part of the 'goodness of God' for granted** and they do not think twice about enjoying God's sunrise and sunset, cool breeze, sleep, eating food, relaxing, walking around, traveling, the joy of family life, children, friends and the freedom to walk away from people you do not like. This is just to name a few of God's goodness on earth but **hell is a place where these things are lacking because God, His presence, goodness, love and mercy, etc., are not there.**

Therefore, if you find yourself there, **you can never come out and you will suffer in anguish forever.** Again, the reason hell lacks these things is because **they all come from God** and **saying no to Him in Christ**, means saying **no to these good things!** The souls in hell are still in God's awareness but not in His presence or His light.

Man's Soul is Activated by God to Live Forever

A soul is defined as the spiritual or immaterial part of a human being; your soul is **the essence of who you are.** Man consists of a **Spirit, Soul** and **Body.** When God created Adam, He gave Adam a body but **Adam was not alive to God** until **God put His breath** *(His Spirit)* **in him** — Genesis 2:7:

> "And **the LORD God formed man of the dust of the ground,** and **breathed into his nostrils the breath of life**; and **man became a Living Soul.**"

God's Breath became the Life in Adam. God activated the spirit and soul of man with **His own Breath** *(spirit)* **and it made Adam a part of God with a Soul that is** <u>alive</u> **forever.** In **Romans 11:29,** we are told that **God's gifts are forever; meaning that His Breath activated the soul of man forever;** man's soul can never die <u>spiritually</u>!

> "**The gifts and the calling of God are without repentance.**"

The soul is the part of a person that **feels and thinks** *(the part you cannot see)*; meaning where we house **our thoughts, our** emotions, our feelings and determine our actions. Being made alive, Adam was given a free will to choose good but with the commandment to obey God's Word forever or die as result of disobedience; any disobedience joins man to the devil and leads to death. Man's soul never dies and it is where we choose **obedience or disobedience** to God's commandments. The human body merely follows wherever the soul leads it.

This is why **the soul is the part of man that God holds accountable for all his actions** while on earth. **It is the part of a person that lives forever representing the whole person.** If the soul received the atoning works of the Lord Jesus, it goes to Heaven but if it did not make Jesus its Lord, it **goes to hell** until the **Day of Judgment.** It must be held accountable for its action and its ways — **Romans 14:12:**

> "...Every one of us shall give account of himself to God."

Every soul is alive to God and it is why the Lord Jesus said in **Matthew 22:31-32,** that **God is the God of the Living:**

> "But as touching the resurrection of the dead, have ye not read that which was spoken unto you by God, saying, 32 **I am the God of Abraham, and the God of Isaac, and the God of Jacob? God is not the God of the dead, but of the living.**"

Therefore, when a person dies, the spirit *(God's Breath)* returns to God and the body returns to the earth where it came from according to God's judgment in **Genesis 3:19:**

> "In the sweat of thy face shalt thou eat bread, till thou return unto the ground; for out of it wast thou taken: **for dust thou art, and unto dust shalt thou return.**"

The **soul is immediately held responsible for its ways and actions** while it was in the body and it must **give account of** his or her actions to God. There is **no part of God that can die** and we are told in **Ecclesiastes 3:14** that:

"…**Whatsover God doeth is forever.**"

Therefore, the **difference between all souls' eternal existence is location, location, location — Heaven or hell! The souls that received God's atonement for their sins will be rewarded with eternal life for believing in God's Son.** All humanity *(Adam's seed)*, was alive in Adam once but we died spiritually because of Adam's sin. **The reason why God placed us on earth is to again be <u>made alive and reconnected</u> with Him in Christ.** The souls who are not made alive are sent to hell and their spiritual bodies will join them there to be tormented and burn forever. Know therefore that everyone will get a new spiritual body to live on in Heaven or hell.

Hell is God's Garbage Disposal

God is a farmer and **<u>every farmer has a place to burn up his garbage</u>; in God's case, it is hell.** We see this in **John 15:1-6:**

"I am the true vine, and my Father is the husbandman. 2 Every branch in me that beareth not fruit he taketh away: and every branch that beareth fruit, he purgeth it, that it may bring forth more fruit…6 <u>If a man abide not in me</u>, he is cast forth as a branch, and is withered; and <u>men gather them, and cast them into the fire, and they are burned</u>."

Those in **hell** will burn forever and they will also **<u>inhale the putrefying smell of sulphur</u>, the <u>smell of their own rotting flesh</u>** *(their decaying bodies and those of demons)* and they can never escape from it. In addition, they will be **tormented by demons as they burn without relief, without water to quench their thirst and without the gentle breeze or fresh air of God that will never blow on them again.** Can you imagine never drinking water again forever but you are very thirsty? Remember that the rich man who refused to show compassion on the beggar Lazarus in **Luke 16:22-24** was thirsty in hell:

> "And it came to pass, that the beggar *(Lazarus)* died, and was carried by the angels into Abraham's bosom: the rich man also died, and was buried; 23 And in hell he lift up his eyes, being in torments, and seeth Abraham afar off, and Lazarus in his bosom 24 **And he cried and said, Father Abraham, have mercy on me, and send Lazarus, that he may dip the tip of his finger in water, and cool my tongue; for I am tormented in this flame.**"

According to reports, **the rich are exceptionally miserable** in hell because they enjoyed the finer things in life while they were on earth. I reiterate that hell is a terrible place to go to because of the following facts:

- The fire in hell will never be quenched
- The worms on the wicked never die— "Where their worms dieth not, and the fire is not quenched" (Mark 9:44)
- Those in hell are cut-off from God and His mercy forever
- Those in hell are tormented by demons day and night
- There is no peace for those in hell
- Everyone in hell is wicked according to the Word of God

From Hell to the Lake of Fire

We learn in **Revelation 20:11-15**, that **it will get worse for all those in hell because <u>they will be cast into the Lake of Fire</u>** when they come before the **Judgment Seat of Christ**:

> "And I saw a **great white throne**, and **<u>him that sat on it</u>** *(the Lord Jesus)*, from whose face the earth and the Heaven fled away; and there was found no place for them. 12 And **I saw the dead, small and great, stand before God**; and the books were opened: and another book was opened, which is the book of life:

and **the dead were judged out of those things which were written in the books, according to their works.** 13 And the sea gave up the dead which were in it; and death and hell delivered up the dead which were in them: and they were judged every man according to their works. 14 And **death and hell were cast into the lake of fire**. This is **the second death** *(eternal separation from God)*. 15 And **whosoever was not found written in the book of life** *(book of all those who believed in Christ)* **was cast into the lake of fire.**"

During the Millennial Reign of Christ, those in hell will be shown to the rest of humanity as **abominations and examples of why not to rebel against God.** Meaning that, **God will display them as a deterrence to anyone who will want to rebel against Him in the age to come** — Isaiah 66:23-24:

"And it shall come to pass, that from one new moon to another, and from one sabbath to another, shall all flesh come to worship before me, saith the LORD. 24 And they shall go forth, and **look upon the carcases of the men that have transgressed against me: for their worm shall not die, neither shall their fire be quenched; and they shall be an abhorring unto all flesh.**"

How to Avoid Hell
- **Accept God's Gift of Salvation in Christ**; only His Blood can wash away your sin
- Discipline yourself to **walk in the fear of God** by obeying or living according to His Word in the Bible
- Meditate on the Lord Jesus' drastic measure in **Matthew 18:8-9:**

"Wherefore if thy hand or thy foot offend thee, cut them off, and cast them from thee: **it is better for thee to enter into life halt or maimed, rather than having two hands or two feet to be cast into everlasting fire.**

9 And if thine eye offend thee, pluck it out, and cast it from thee: **it is better for thee to enter into life with one eye, rather than having two eyes to be cast into hell fire."**

- In other words, **discipline yourself drastically to stay away from acts of sin**

Conclusion

The whole purpose of this book is to encourage you and let you know that it is not too late to make the Lord Jesus your Savior even after Rapture has occurred. It does not matter what religion you practiced before Rapture occurred but you must now make Him your Lord. Now is the time for you to act upon what you have read in this book that the Lord Jesus is the only Way to God as He said in **John 14:6:**

> "Jesus saith unto him, **I am the way, the truth, and the life: no man cometh unto the Father, but by Me."**

And in **John 10:7-11:**

> "Then said Jesus unto them again, Verily, verily, I say unto you, I am the door *(the only Way to God)* of the sheep *(Believers)*. 8 All that ever came before me are thieves and robbers *(false religious leaders)*: but the sheep did not hear them. 9 **I am the door: by me if any man enter in, he shall be saved, and shall go in and out, and find pasture.**
>
> 10 **The thief** *(the devil)* **cometh not, but for to steal, and to kill, and to destroy: I am come that they** *(you)* **might have life, and that they might have it more abundantly.** 11 I am the good shepherd: **the good shepherd giveth his life for the sheep** *(He died for your sins)."*

If You Practiced another Religion before Rapture

The fact that God Almighty came and took away those who placed their trust in Him should serve as a reminder to you that there is only one God and His Son is Jesus Christ. He is the only Savior of the world! You just read this in the above scriptures and it was confirmed by the occurrence of the Rapture.

Remember that you were left behind because you did not place your trust in Him. Instead, you practiced a religion that He did not approve of. Today, you are the very confirmation that only those who follow the Lord Jesus can obtain Salvation and avoid condemnation to hell when they die. **God did not place His Salvation in Islam, Hinduism, Buddhism, Jehovah's Witness, Mormonism, animism, paganism, ancestral worship, new age, occultism, or any other religion.**

The name of Jesus Christ is the only name that Almighty God gave to save all humanity. You can read this again in **Acts 4:12:**

> "Neither is there salvation in any other: **for there is none other name under heaven given among men** *(all humanity)*, **whereby we must be saved.**"

I repeated the steps and **Prayer of Salvation below for those that want to ask the Lord Jesus for forgiveness of their sins and make Him the Lord and Savior of their souls.** When you ask Jesus Christ to be your Lord and you mean it, it is something that no one can take from you and **do not renounce Him even when they want to kill you physically because all who do, will be condemned to hell.**

It is critical that <u>you believe in the Lord Jesus and make Him your Lord with the prayer below</u> before you put this book down. Time is of the essence for you right now.

The Steps and Message of Salvation

To receive the Lord Jesus as your Savior, you must first believe the **Good News** of the Word of God in **John 3:16-18:**

> "**For God so loved the world, that he gave his only begotten Son, that whosoever believeth in him should not perish, but have everlasting life.** For God sent not his Son into the world to condemn the world; but that the world through him might be saved. *18* **He that believeth on him is not condemned: but <u>he that believeth not is condemned already</u>,** because he hath not believed in the name of the only begotten Son of God."

You must also believe that **the Lord Jesus is the Only Way that you can get to God in Heaven as stated in Romans 10:9-10:**

> **"That if thou shalt confess with thy mouth the Lord Jesus, and shalt believe in thine heart that God hath raised him from the dead, thou shalt be saved.** *10* For with the heart man believeth unto righteousness; and with the mouth confession is made unto salvation."

Pray the Prayer below **aloud if you believe** what is written in the Scriptures above:

The Prayer of Salvation

"Father, in the name of the Lord Jesus, I come to you and **I believe that Jesus Christ is Your Son. I believe that He came into the world in the flesh and that He was crucified on the Cross for my sins. He died on the Cross for my sins and was buried but on the third day, You raised Him from the dead.**

Today, I confess it with my mouth and I believe it in my heart. Lord Jesus, **I repent of all my sins, I ask You to forgive me all my sins and wash me of my sins with Your blood. Please, come into my heart and be my Lord** for I surrender to Your Lordship this day and forever. Give me Your eternal life for I declare that I belong to You from now on.

Also, I ask You to **give me Your Holy Spirit** to keep me in Your will, teach me the Bible, lead and protect me. I choose to do only those things that please You from now on. Father, I believe that You heard me and that I am now your child. Thank You for giving me Your Son and Your Holy Spirit. I receive them in the name of the Lord Jesus; Amen."

It is a big deal to make the Lord Jesus your Lord and Savior so, congratulations if you just prayed the Prayer of Salvation and meant it from your heart. **Believing in Jesus Christ is a matter of spending eternity in heaven and not hell. God bless you — Prophetess Mary O.**

Books by Prophetess Mary Ogenaarekhua

Books by Prophetess Mary Ogenaarekhua

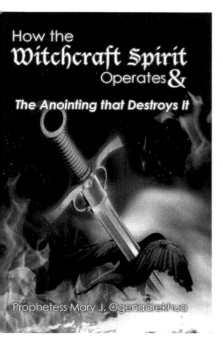

Books by Prophetess Mary Ogenaarekhua

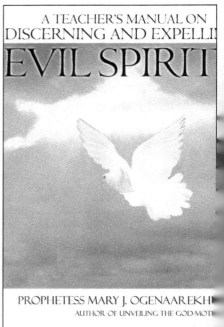

Books by Prophetess Mary Ogenaarekhua

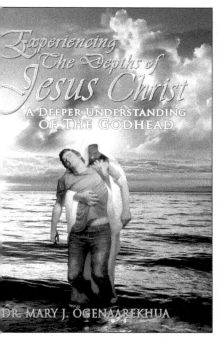

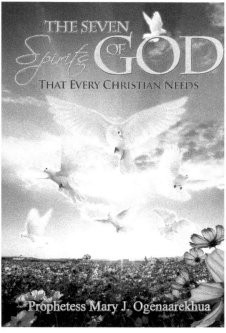

CPSIA information can be obtained
at www.ICGtesting.com
Printed in the USA
JSHW011419270523
42349JS00001B/4